ERIC TEACHER EDUCATION MONOGRAPH NO. 1

USING RESEARCH TO IMPROVE TEACHER EDUCATION

THE NEBRASKA CONSORTIUM

Robert L. Egbert
Mary M. Kluender

Volume Editors

Published by

CLEARINGHOUSE
ON TEACHER
EDUCATION

American Association of Colleges for Teacher Education
Teachers College, University of Nebraska–Lincoln

March 1984

i

CITE AS:

Egbert, Robert L., & Kluender, Mary M. (Eds.). (1984). *Using Research to Improve Teacher Education: The Nebraska Consortium.* (Teacher Education Monograph No. 1). Washington, DC: ERIC Clearinghouse on Teacher Education.

MANUSCRIPTS:

The ERIC Clearinghouse on Teacher Education invites individuals to submit proposals for writing monographs for the Teacher Education Monograph Series. Proposals must include:

1. A detailed manuscript proposal of not more than five pages.
2. A 75-word summary to be used by reviewers for the initial screening and rating of each proposal.
3. A vita.
4. A writing sample.

ORDERS:

The price for a single copy, including Fourth Class postage and handling, is $6.50. For First Class postage, add $.60 for each copy ordered. Orders must be prepaid.

ISBN 0–89333–031–0

ERIC CLEARINGHOUSE ON TEACHER EDUCATION
American Association of Colleges for Teacher Education
One Dupont Circle, N.W., Suite 610
Washington, D.C. 20036
(202) 293-2450

Series Editor: Elizabeth A. Asburn, Director of the ERIC Clearinghouse on Teacher Education and AACTE Information Services

This publication received partial support for printing costs from the Mid-Continent Regional Educational Laboratory (McREL); however, points of view or opinions expressed in this volume do not necessarily reflect the views of McREL.

This publication was prepared with funding from the National Institute of Education, U.S. Department of Education under Contract No. 400-83-0022. The opinions expressed in this report do not necessarily reflect the positions or policies of NIE or DOE.

Preface

The Teachers College, University of Nebraska–Lincoln, is pleased to serve as a sponsor for USING RESEARCH TO IMPROVE TEACHER EDUCATION: THE NEBRASKA CONSORTIUM. It is our hope that this volume will be of value to teacher educators throughout the country in their continuing efforts to enhance the quality of teacher education.

Our interest in the activities which led to this volume is two-fold. First, we believe that the consortium concept is a most important approach to the improvement of teacher education. The Nebraska Consortium has brought together representatives of all the teacher education programs in Nebraska to learn through sharing experiences with each other and with persons who have conducted research important to the education of teachers. We believe that this joint work benefits all of the programs in our state. In these days of frequent public criticism of teacher education, it is important that teacher educators study their programs thoroughly, developing carefully reasoned responses to these criticisms. The Consortium provides a proper setting for such study.

Our second interest in the work reported here is the emphasis on research as a foundation for teacher education. Clearly, teacher education as well as teaching itself is both an art and a science. An analysis of current practice, however, will most likely reveal that less attention is paid to the use of science in the development and conduct of teacher education than is needed. The papers presented in this volume are addressed to that need. It is our goal in Teachers College to provide as much support as we can for the development of a broader research and theory base for the conduct of teacher education.

James P. O'Hanlon
Dean, Teachers College

USING RESEARCH TO IMPROVE TEACHER EDUCATION THE NEBRASKA CONSORTIUM

Contents

The Nebraska Consortium: Using Research to Improve Teacher Education

Mary M. Kluender

University of Nebraska-Lincoln

INTRODUCTION

During the past ten years, there has been a major increase in the amount and quality of research on teaching, learning and effective schools. Research on how teachers plan and make judgments in the classroom about individual students and instructional strategies (Shavelson, 1983), how teachers organize and manage their classrooms (Brophy, 1983), and how they utilize their instructional time (Denham & Lieberman, 1980), are examples of research areas which have developed enough in the last decade to provide serious guidance to the classroom teacher. Education now has the beginnings of a research base upon which to make decisions rather than relying solely upon practices acquired through the experiences of individuals or teachers as a group.

Although the research base itself has expanded, the results of that research have been implemented only to a limited degree, either in the classroom or in the training of teachers. One of the accusations that has frequently been made against teacher education is that it does not use a theoretical, research-based body of knowledge in its training programs, thus perpetuating the practice of teaching as a craft rather than as a profession. For example, B. O. Smith, in *Design for a School of Pedagogy* (1980), suggests that although the research on general concepts, principles and skills of teaching and classroom management has grown and become more dependable, there is reason to believe a large portion of the education faculty in most institutions teaches with little knowledge or utilization of that research. Others support Smith's position and emphasize the need to incorporate the research base into the preservice education of teachers (e.g., Denemark et al., 1982).

To accomplish such a change, however, a mechanism is needed through which institutions and individual faculty members can examine and change some of their own knowledge and behaviors. One approach to the improvement of teacher education programs has been to increase external controls, either through mandated competency testing programs or legislation. For example, at least 20 states have adopted some requirement for competency

1

testing of teacher education graduates (Ashburn & Strauss, 1981); in Florida, the state has adopted a detailed set of competencies for all teachers (draft, Office of Teacher Education, Florida, 1983); Georgia has adopted the Georgia Teacher Certificate test, and several states are using the National Teacher Examination. In each case, the measures are externally imposed, and there appears to be little evidence of active involvement of the institutions which educate those teachers. An alternative approach to statewide improvement, which is described in this document, is initiation and implementation of improvement efforts by the institutions themselves.

The Consortium of Teacher Education Model

In June, 1983, the fifteen Nebraska institutions of higher education with teacher education programs formed the Nebraska Consortium for the Improvement of Teacher Education, with the goal of improving teacher education by facilitating the introduction of research findings into their programs. More specifically, the Consortium members discussed the following long-range outcomes:

1. Develop a network of teacher education institutions that will work in close cooperation toward the improvement of teacher education in their state.
2. Increase faculty members' confidence in and knowledge of the research base to the extent that they will use appropriate portions of that base in their own programs.
3. Change the nature of teacher education programs in participating institutions so that they will be more amenable to use of the teaching/ learning and effective schools base.
4. Develop faculty members' willingness to study research publications alone and with other faculty groups and to build the results of their study into their programs.
5. Develop in students the knowledge of, the confidence in, and skills in working with the research base such that they will draw upon that base both during their teacher education programs and in their teaching assignments.
6. Affect the schools at which the students do their student teaching such that the faculty of those schools will have both a positive attitude toward the research base and skill in using it.

As its first major activity, the Consortium decided to hold a workshop on the utilization of research on teaching and learning in teacher education programs. The University of Nebraska-Lincoln agreed to organize and manage the workshop; each of the fifteen institutions agreed to establish a team which would attend the workshop and develop a plan of action based on the workshop sessions. This monograph is drawn from that workshop.

Team Formation

The dean or head of each teacher education program selected a team of 3-6 faculty members to attend the workshop. In most cases, team members were selected because of their key positions in the undergraduate teacher education program, their interest in research and the incorporation of research into their courses, and their ability to provide leadership for program change. In some cases, because of the size of the teacher education program, the team represented a substantial portion of the total education faculty. In other instances, the team was a cross-section of a much larger faculty who would need to be informed and involved after the workshop was completed and the initial plans had been developed.

Activities Prior to the Workshop

Before attending the workshop, the team members were asked to do some preparatory reading. Each institution was provided a set of materials which included papers by several leading researchers on teaching, learning and effective schools, publications on the effective utilization of time, and a bibliography of other references. About two months before the workshop was held, each institution also was asked to provide background information about its teacher education program, including such materials as a current college bulletin, requirements for graduation in the teacher education program, and syllabi from several key teacher education courses. A preliminary analysis of that information was done prior to the workshop; after further analysis, a report will be developed for the Consortium institutions about the status of teacher education programs in Nebraska.

Workshop Structure and Activities

The two-and-one-half day workshop was planned with several goals in mind. First, team members who attended the workshop should have an opportunity to read and discuss the research and to have contact with a few of the researchers who have made important contributions to some of the influential research efforts. Second, teams should have an opportunity to consider the research in relationship to their own teacher education programs. Third, the workshop should provide a setting which might lead to informal networks among institutions, which could be helpful as institutions implemented their plans. To accomplish those goals, the workshop provided time for presentations on research, discussion among institutions, and institutional planning. The first day emphasized mastery of research, discussion of implications, and dialogue among participants; the second day emphasized team discussion and planning.

Three types of presentations were included in the workshop: (1) two presentations analyzed the task of incorporating research into practice from the perspective of several audiences; (2) six presentations analyzed specific portions of the research in some detail; and (3) three presentations broadly synthesized the research and discussed the implications of that research for teaching and teacher education practice.

The two presentations that focused on implementation methodology were made by people who are directly involved in implementation activities with inservice teachers. Their presentations included both discussions of strategy and analysis of the meaning of incorporation of research findings into teachers' classroom practice.

Lovely Billups, from the American Federation of Teachers, discussed the traditional gap between research and classroom practice and described an innovative approach that AFT has undertaken to help teachers incorporate some of the research findings into their classrooms. That strategy, which utilizes Teacher Research Linkers as the means of working with other teachers, is described in her paper.

Robert Ewy and *Linda Sikorski,* staff members of the Midcontinent Regional Educational Laboratory (McREL), described McREL's Effective Schools Program, a research dissemination and utilization effort in a seven state region, and their strategy for evaluating the extent of implementation and the impact of the training upon teacher behavior, school behavior and student outcomes.

Six workshop sessions on specific research topics were presented in concurrent sessions, one set in the morning and one in the afternoon, during the the first day of the workshop. Teams were encouraged to distribute member attendance across the sessions for broader coverage of the topics. The six papers were written independently, but they contain a number of important interrelationships, at times drawing upon the same research base, and at other times addressing similar classroom concerns from different perspectives. Together, they provide the reader with a useful entry into a complex and varied body of research.

Roger Bruning has analyzed a body of research that has become known as "Direct Teaching." He notes that during the past decade

> a large and substantial body of information, based on converging lines of evidence, has provided support for the contention that instructional techniques *do* have important effects on the outcomes of learning, most particularly on the achievement levels of students who experience the instruction.

Based on the work of researchers such as Kounin, Rosenshine, Good, Brophy and Stallings, Bruning summarizes the characteristics of effective teachers in a Direct Teaching Model, and suggests that those characteristics involve skills that can be taught to preservice teachers.

Alvah Kilgore, in his paper "Models of Teaching and Teacher Education," uses Joyce and Weil's *Models of Teaching* as a framework for analyzing teaching strategies, and examines the research base for several of those models. Kilgore, like Joyce and Weil, believes that teachers must acquire a broad

4

repertoire of teaching skills and models and the diagnostic skill to decide the appropriate use of those models.

James Walter reviews the literature on research on teacher planning and decision making. In his analysis, Walter observes that teachers do not follow the planning models often advocated by curriculum planners and taught in preservice courses, which emphasize planning from goals; instead, teacher planning typically is based on specific instructional tasks and, once instruction is in place, teachers are reluctant to change. Like Kilgore, Walter believes that one of the tasks of teacher education is to help teachers to expand the number of alternative instructional strategies upon which they can draw.

Stanley Vasa reviews the research done in the area of classroom management. While Bruning, Kilgore and Walter focus on the teacher's instructional strategies and decisions, Vasa's review concentrates on management of behaviors related to maintenance of on-task behaviors and reduction of disruptive behaviors in the classroom. Drawing heavily on Kounin, Vasa summarizes research findings on effective teacher management behavior beginning with planning prior to the school year, during instruction, and in response to disruptive behavior.

Toni Santmire and Patricia Friesen analyze teacher-child interactions in the classroom from the perspective of developmental psychology. They argue that if teachers are to provide optimum learning for students, they must understand the nature of the developmental differences at different ages, and ways in which those characteristics affect how the student will respond to the instructional environment. They then examine the effective schools research in light of what is known about developmental characteristics of students at different stages and why successful instruction and management techniques change as the child grows older.

Robert Egbert and *Mary Kluender* review the considerable body of literature that has developed on the utilization of time in the classroom. They describe the concept of Academic Learning Time, as used in the Beginning Teacher Evaluation Study (BTES), examine several other large-scale studies as well as a number of smaller studies of the effects of time allocation and utilization on student achievement and other academic outcomes, and propose some implications for schools and teacher education that emerge from the time to learn concept.

Three of the sessions, which were distributed throughout the conference, served an integrative and synthesizing role. They provided structure to the workshop, drew some principles from the more specific sessions, and raised some philosophical and policy-related questions for team members to consider as they made decisions about which research to incorporate into their programs and what strategies to use as they work toward incorporation of that research.

Robert Egbert, in the workshop's opening presentation, provided both a rationale for the Consortium effort and a description of the workshop's structure. In his paper, Egbert compares educators' attitudes toward the use of educational and social science research to those in other professions, and

5

finds education, and teacher education, far less willing to apply research findings to practice. He describes some areas of potential congruence between bodies of educational research and the content of teacher education programs, and identifies several specific research areas which were the focus of this workshop.

Gary Fenstermacher, from Virginia Polytechnical Institute, provided the mid-point synthesizing presentation, in which he discussed the premises from which teachers operate, and the ways in which teacher educators can help teachers examine those premises and use research findings as a means of validating or revising those premises. In his paper, Fenstermacher contends that teacher educators play an important role in conveying and fostering a manner, or pattern of behavior, among preservice teachers by modeling positive intellectual and educational traits.

Jane Stallings, in the last large group presentation, synthesized much of the research that was presented in detail in the six content sessions, discussed the implications of that research for the teacher in the classroom, and suggested ways in which the research findings could be incorporated into the education of preservice teachers.

Discussion sessions were interspersed among the workshop presentations, to allow workshop participants opportunity to ask questions and talk about the implications of the research findings for teacher education programs in general, and in their own institutions. By the end of the first day of the conference, teams began to meet separately for institutional planning.

Action Plans and
Future Consortium Activities

When the workshop was first planned, it was agreed that by the end of the workshop, each institutional team would have developed an Initial Action Plan to take back to their institution for review, revision and implementation. The last portion of the workshop was devoted to the development of those plans, which are described in this document. Once revised, those action plans are to serve as guides for implementation.

A secondary goal of the consortium was to foster interrelationships among the fifteen institutions. Several steps are being taken to foster those interrelationships. First, a copy of each institution's Initial Action Plan will be sent to every other institution. Second, a fall, 1984 meeting of the Consortium teams will be held, at which time the teams will report progress on their plans. A third step will also be initiated at that time, which is for the group to decide upon future improvement activities which the Consortium might sponsor that will support the implementation of the action plans and other improvement activities.

Summary

Teacher education programs are influenced to a large extent by the state of which they are a part. The state, through its certification and accreditation processes, its legislation and its regulatory powers, plays a significant role in the nature of the requirements preservice teachers must meet and the courses or programs they must take. In some states, this regulatory function is quite explicit and detailed; in others, the institutions have more leeway within the state's guidelines. But in all cases, the teacher education programs in both public and private institutions are influenced to some degree by the policies, philosophy and the character of the state in which they reside.

Teacher education programs also are influenced by the institutions of which they are a part. An institution's teacher education program reflects the philosophy and values of the larger institution, the characteristics of its faculty and students, and the clientele which the program serves. Thus, within one state, institutions which operate within the same state guidelines will approach teacher education from quite different perspectives.

At the same time that teacher education programs are subject to the requirements and influences of the state and the academic institutions of which they are a part, they can, in turn, exert considerable influence upon those organizational structures. One of the ways that they can influence those structures is by explaining and interpreting the knowledge base in education. As the primary source of knowledge about educational research, members of the teacher education community have a responsibility to bring the perspective of the research base to bear upon the current debate about improvement in education, both to assist in improving the complex teaching/learning process and to inform policymakers as they consider alternative improvement policies.

The Nebraska Consortium for the Improvement of Teacher Education was established with these factors in mind. The Consortium members recognize that any attempts to improve the state's teacher education programs must take into consideration both the state's and the institution's goals and characteristics, as well as knowledge about teacher education and effective schooling.

References

Ashburn, E., & Strauss, M. B. (1981). *A survey of competency assessment activities of land grant colleges of teacher education, November, 1980.* Ohio State University.

Brophy, J. (1983). Classroom organization and management. *Elementary School Journal, 83*, 265-285.

Denemark, G. et al. (1982). *Educating a profession: Profile of a beginning teacher.*

Washington, DC: American Association of Colleges for Teacher Education.

Denham, C., & Lieberman, A. (1980). *Time to learn.* Washington, DC: National Institute of Education.

Florida, Office of Teacher Education. (1983). *Handbook of the Florida performance measurement system.* Tallahassee, FL: Florida Beginning Teacher Program.

Shavelson, R. (1983). Review of research on teachers' pedagogical judgments, plans, and decisions. *Elementary School Journal, 83,* 392-413.

Smith, B. O. (1980). *A design for a school of pedagogy.* Washington, DC: Government Printing Office.

The Role of
Research in Teacher Education

Robert L. Egbert

University of Nebraska-Lincoln

E ducation did not find itself in March of 1983 under sudden attack from newspapers, news magazines, taxpayers and parents. Instead, there has been a gradually rising flow of criticism that more than once has seemed to have reached high tide and then begun to ebb, only to be pushed forward by some new current. At the same time that critics have attacked education, friends have defended us, and the effect has been mixed. The most recent maelstrom of controversy about education has as its primary origin *A NATION AT RISK*, the report of the Commission on Excellence in Education. Newspapers, news magazines, and many members of the public have picked up on the findings, discussion and recommendations of *A NATION AT RISK* and other reports and concluded the worst about our schools, our school personnel and the institutions that educate them. Often out of pride and frustration and occasionally from ignorance or indolence, we have reacted defensively and sometimes complacently. *These responses are natural, but inadequate.* We must correct misinformation. We cannot stand idly by while ill-informed and occasionally badly motivated critics attack those institutions and people responsible for educating our youth; but we also must show that we know that even the best can improve, and we must show a willingness to do so.

One dimension on which we in education lag behind most other professions is in the conduct of research and the systematic use of information produced by research. (For a much more complete discussion of the potential role of research [inquiry] in education, see Gideonse, 1983.) Because the intent of this paper is to deal with how the interaction between teacher education and research can help improve the performance of our profession, it is organized around three topics: (1) the role of research in education, (2) the content and structure of teacher education, and (3) an effort at program improvement in teacher education through the use of research information.

Research and Education

The practice of any profession, whether that profession is engineering, architecture, medicine, agriculture or education, is dependent on information from at least three sources—the experience of the individual professional, the accumulated experience of the profession, and research. Each profession has a different history of how its members put information from these three sources together and each one has a different history of research and development activities. Furthermore, each profession has had a set of obstacles to overcome in order for research to assume an appropriate role as a source of information to assist in professional practice.

Like other professions, education has its own special problems related to the conduct and utilization of research. Two brief incidents, taken together, represent much of what underlies our present problematic circumstance in the conduct and use of research in education. The first incident happened several years ago at a major university in the home state of the chairman of the Senate Appropriations Committee, a senator who was openly derisive of the National Institute of Education and who on more than one occasion recommended zero funding for it. This same senator strongly supported research in other fields. At dinner one evening, I was seated by a university education faculty member who was politically associated with the senator. Thinking that this was an opportunity to help secure support for NIE, I mentioned the senator's opposition and suggested that the faculty member might enlist his support for research in education. Her response was, "Oh, I know that he is opposed to NIE. So am I. NIE doesn't do anything for us. And, besides, research isn't important in education anyway."

The second incident occurred at a meeting in which a junior high school principal spoke harshly about teacher education—much more harshly than appeared either accurate or appropriate. When I remonstrated, he related the following experience. He was invited to speak to a group of teacher education seniors who were ready to begin student teaching. His assignment was to discuss with them research information that he had found useful in his junior high school, but he didn't want to bore them by reviewing research that they already knew so he asked that they signal when he touched on familiar material. He began by discussing Ben Bloom's taxonomy and mastery learning ideas. Two or three hands went up. He continued with Joe Hunt's research on the importance of learning and development during the first few years of life. Still, two or three hands. Then he went on to the Anderson, Evertson, Brophy, and Emmer classroom management research and to the Beginning Teacher Evaluation Study and other research on time to learn. All evidence of prior familiarity disappeared. The junior high school principal's conclusion was that if the research is old enough to appear in the standard textbooks, some of our students may be introduced to it; if the research is so recent as to be only in the journals or other current publications, almost none of them will even have heard of it.

In order to obtain added insight about one profession, it is sometimes useful to consider it in relation to another profession. To permit achieving the insight that may come from such a comparison, I should like to divert our attention from education to another field, to illustrate how research can change the manner in which the professional in the field functions. The field that I have chosen is agriculture.

Historically, we have not thought of the farmer as a professional. In fact, even in Nebraska where agriculture forms the state's economic base, being called a farmer often is not considered a mark of approbation. But more and more, the farmer is a professional, an agriculturist, a person who must have extensive knowledge that is based on research—in diseases, economics, plant and animal breeding, soils, climatology, and technology—and must use that knowledge in increasingly complex and integrated ways in order to be successful. So let's consider the agricultural professional, the 1980s farmer and along with that farmer, the educational professional, the 1980s teacher, or teacher educator.

In the past, most of us have thought of the farmer as a person who tasted the soil to determine its acidity, employed a diviner to locate the best place to dig a well, held up an index finger to determine the wind's direction, prayed for rain or sunshine, and worked from dawn till dark. This farmer learned his trade from his father, serving a two-decade apprenticeship. What he knew, he learned from that apprenticeship. In 1983, the pattern is different. The successful farmer has attended a first rate, well-funded university. He or she has studied chemistry, physics, biology, history, sociology, and economics, and the applications of those sciences to agriculture. 1980s farmers have personal computers to receive up-to-the-minute weather and market reports and to tell them when to turn their quarter section, pivot irrigation systems on and off, and sometimes to do it for them. These farmers drive massive, complicated tractors and harvesters while sitting in air conditioned, stereo-equipped cabs; they recognize potential disease problems in plants and animals, and they know the chemical properties of the herbicides and fertilizers that they use and the implications of those properties. They know the characteristics of weeds and soils, they know the intricacies and the implications of soil erosion, and they know about nature's aquifers that store their water. The science that these farmers draw upon began in the laboratories and other work places of biochemists, atomic physicists, geneticists, botanists and economists. Knowledge gained in these fields was transformed and tested by applied scientists in agriculture, in their specialized laboratories and experimental herds and field plots. Finally, they were field tested on farms and ranches for feasibility and practicability and the information was made available through a nationwide Cooperative Extension Service. Successful farmers of the 1980s keep current on the implications of field tested developments and they know enough of the underpinning science to be able to interpret more than just the conclusions.

Successful farmers of the 1980s also have served a kind of apprentice-ship, both before and after they completed their university education. These farmers synthesize the science of the classroom with the experience gained from day to day, season to season work with corn and cattle, wheat and turkeys, soil and water. To the extent that they successfully synthesize knowl-edge from these quite different sources, they become successful; the farmer who relies too heavily on knowledge from one source or the other, ultimately will fall short of his or her potential.

Farming has changed dramatically during the past fifty years—even during the past five to ten years. *For example, even though the number of persons employed on Nebraska's farms has decreased more than twenty percent in just the last five years, production has continued to increase.* These counter-trends have resulted from farmers' ability to synthesize the information from their sci-entific knowledge base with that from their experiential knowledge base and to use and continue to test that knowledge in the real world of farming. No farmer, any more than a teacher, a physician, or an architect, simply applies what he or she reads in an extension service bulletin. The farmer reads, ponders, adapts, applies, evaluates, and modifies—just as any other profes-sional does.

In every realm, not just in agriculture, present day society has been enriched by efforts of scientists and scholars. Space travel, nuclear power, the green revolution, organ transplants, friendly microcomputers, and the elim-ination of measles, diptheria, and poliomyletus all have come about through research coupled with powerful systems for keeping users appropriately in-formed. Like other fields, education depends for its progress on developing new knowledge and converting that knowledge to usable materials and proc-esses and then making those materials and processes available to teachers, administrators, other school personnel and to educational policymakers so that they can study them, test them in their own ways and situations as profes-sionals do in other fields and then use them as appropriate. Preschool edu-cation, classroom management, the teaching of reading and mathematics, the use of instructional time, and the teaching of handicapped children are examples of education areas in which research has begun to build a sizeable knowledge base during the past few years.

* Federal and state-level policymakers have been sufficiently informed by longitudinal studies that they can be confident that well-planned and con-ducted preschool programs for at risk children will be both personally and socially beneficial as well as financially sound investments (Weikart & Schweinhart, 1979; Darlington, 1982).

* Through classroom management and time for learning research and de-velopment activities, teachers and administrators have been provided infor-mation and materials that they can use in improving overall efficiency and effectiveness of classrooms and schools (Denham & Lieberman, 1980; AASA, 1982; Brophy, 1983).

* Extensive research has demonstrated that direct instruction techniques are highly successful for increasing the early grades achievement of children from

12

low-income families (Stebbins, St. Pierre, Proper, Anderson & Cerva; Bereiter & Kurland, 1978; Rosenshine, 1983).

Until the middle 1970s almost all of the available evidence suggested that when at risk children experienced good preschool programs, they made immediate gains in IQ that placed them somewhat higher than similar children who did not attend preschool but that when they and similar children entered school the IQ differences disappeared. Furthermore, the large-scale Westinghouse study of Headstart graduates was interpreted as demonstrating that Headstart had no lasting educational benefits. Most of these early studies focused on IQ and standardized achievement test scores. However, when long-term follow-up studies were conducted of at risk children from high quality preschool programs of the 1960s, some of the researchers considered multiple behavioral and social outcomes. On the behavioral and social indices, substantial and significant differences have been found on measures ranging all the way from retention at grade level and assignment to special education classes to delinquency and employment status. This research is of great importance both to early childhood educators and to educational policymakers charged with responsibility for making funding and program decisions (Schweinhart, 1983).

A second example is taken from the "time to learn" research. Simple observation suggests that the more time students (children) spend studying a particular process or content, the more they will learn about it. However, until the last few years, neither researchers nor practitioners paid much attention to this obvious fact. It's true that both states and districts often mandated the amounts of time that should be devoted to specific subject matter areas, but they did little more than mandate. Seldom did anyone seriously follow up to see what happened in actual practice. Twenty years ago, a few educational psychologists began thinking about the issue, but no one set about studying it in detail. Finally, in the middle and late 1970s, the amount of time that was actually spent in teaching and studying began to be researched. Information was produced which suggested that a large portion of school time is not allocated for instruction, that much of the time allocated to instruction is used for non-instructional purposes, and that teachers and administrators can make choices that will increase the amount of time available for student learning (Egbert & Kluender, this volume). This research has immediate and important implications for both teacher education and classroom teaching.

Education also has undergone dramatic changes during the past twenty years. Some of the changes have resulted from court decisions, some from legislation, some from the application of different perspectives, some from a talented sales person creating a novel idea and selling it from coast to coast—and some changes in education have come from research. But the changes that research has wrought in education are not nearly as profound or far reaching as either, (a) the changes produced by research in other fields, or (b) the changes produced in education by other forces.

Although the research base has increased in each of the areas cited, the application of that research has been sporadic at best. The relative immaturity of the sciences upon which we in education have depended most heavily—psychology and sociology—has contributed to the minimal impact of research on our field. Our failure to perform the systematic translations and transformations that must be done from basic science to applied science to field tested products and processes also has diminished that impact. But even where the applied research has been conducted and the practical implications are fairly obvious, we have failed to take advantage of them. For instance, Biles, Billups and Veitch (1983) note in a report of an American Federation of Teachers project to utilize educational research,

> "None of the TRLs (Teacher Research Linkers) trained in the program were familiar with the bodies of research presented. Few used research information as a continuing frame of reference for daily teaching. Most were skeptical of research, stating that it was conflicting, limited and too difficult to wade through.

> By the end of the pilot project, TRLs and teachers they reached reversed those attitudes and began asking 'Is there research on . . .?' TRLs commented in feedback sessions that before the project they never would have looked to research for assistance and that knowing what made for more effective teaching made them think about their own teaching.

> All of the TRLs and most of the teachers they reached indicated a certain renewal of professional pride as a result of the program training activities." (pp. 7-8)

I am convinced that the attitudes represented by the pre-training comments from the AFT group are almost universal among teachers and administrators and among teacher educators. At best, we are skeptical of research processes and information; at worst, we are anti-intellectual.

From what I know of research and research use in agriculture and education, my interpretation is that we suffer by comparison, at each step. The science on which we have relied is not as mature as the science undergirding agriculture; we have not developed as complete a system for the step by step integration and transformation of basic research information to usable applications; we have not taught our preservice students the most recent and applicable research information and how to use it; we have not provided inservice and continuing education that draws substantially on a research base; we have not united to secure the necessary funds for educational research, development and dissemination; and we have failed as a profession to understand and appreciate the importance of research to our field. *We have valued the personal and cumulative experiential knowledge of our profession all out of proportion to that which could be contributed by research,* either research which confirms and illuminates good practice (Smith, 1983) or research that opens the way to improvement in practice beyond the best that we know today.

Research and Teacher Education

R esearch and teacher education have several interactive functions, including the conduct of research by teacher educators. However, the focus of this monograph is the utilization, not the production, of research information in teacher education. To facilitate discussion of the use of research information in teacher education programs, those programs are first described and then the use of research information in them is discussed.

The Content of Teacher Education

Each teacher education program is made up of three major components—general studies, the major field or the content that is taught, and the professional education sequence. The general studies portion of the program usually is very similar, sometimes identical, to that for any other major field in the college or university. That is, teacher education students tend to enroll in the same art, composition and literature courses and the same social and natural science courses as students in English or chemistry or philosophy. For prospective secondary school teachers, the major field also tends to be quite similar to that for students studying the same major but not planning to teach. For prospective elementary teachers, the major field is somewhat more complex. Because most elementary teachers serve in self-contained classrooms and teach everything from reading and mathematics to social studies and science, they complete both some specific content courses such as mathematics, children's literature, and art and a series of methods courses that are, in fact, a combination of curriculum analysis, content for teaching, and teaching methods. In many instances, the major field for elementary teachers is elementary education; in other instances, it may be a separate, subject matter field.

The third portion of the prospective teacher's program, professional education, is, in turn, made up of three parts: undergirding foundations and science courses, curriculum and methods, and field experiences. This portion of the program, which many of our critics view as being the entire program, usually is about 20 percent of a secondary and from 40 to 45 percent of an elementary program.

The foundations and educational science part of the professional program most frequently has three or four courses: introduction to education, human (child or adolescent) development, educational psychology and perhaps one other course—evaluation, philosophy, educational sociology, etc. The field experience usually consists of one semester of full or part time student teaching and one or more pre-student teaching field experiences, plus some field experience in one or more methods or educational science courses. Often, an integrative seminar accompanies student teaching. In secondary education, one or two courses usually comprise the methods part of the professional program; the typical pattern is a special methods course and an additional general methods or curriculum course. In addition, many programs require a reading methods and/or special education course. In elementary education, the most common core of methods courses is reading, mathematics, science, social studies, language arts, art, music, physical education and special education. The average total credits for the three professional education parts of the elementary and secondary programs in a national sample are shown in Table 1 (Kluender and Egbert, 1983).

Table 1

Average Number of Credits for Elementary and
Secondary Teacher Education Programs

Program	Foundations and Education-Related Science	Methods	Field Experiences
Elementary	13.2	30.7	11.3
Secondary	8.6	7.8	10.4

The Application of Research in Teacher Education

Teacher educators should include research information in each of the three general components mentioned earlier—(1) foundations and education-related science, (2) curriculum and methods, and (3) field experiences. For a teacher education program to accommodate extensive new research information, the research must be introduced consistently across the student's multiple experiences. Thus, research information from the foundations and from education-related science should be introduced in the first block of professional courses, its application should be demonstrated and discussed in the curriculum and methods sequence, and it should be applied by the student, with support from the cooperating teacher, in the field experience. Research that documents and explicates the validity of clinical experience (Smith, 1983) as well as research related to the design of new methods and materials may be introduced initially in the curriculum and methods courses, but it also should be applied by the student in field experiences. If this process is followed in sequential steps, there is increased probability that the student not only will learn about the research and be able to apply it but s/he also will have greater appreciation for the value of research to teaching. However, for the sequential experience to occur, teacher educators and cooperating teachers alike must both understand and appreciate the research and must themselves use it in their teaching. Thus, plans for the improvement of teacher education through the utilization of research information must begin with teacher educators and these plans must be comprehensive in their application.

In initial attempts at increased utilization of research information, teacher educators may need to concentrate on a limited and defined portion of the total applicable body of educational research. That is the approach used in this monograph. Figure 1 is a highly simplified separation of the structure of educational research into eight categories in order to facilitate comparison of the portion of educational research reviewed in this document with the total body of such research.

Figure 1 is not intended to be inclusive. In fact, the informality of the sketch is designed to show that it does not attempt to include all of educational research. Furthermore, the separations are recognized as being artificial. They are shown for explanatory purposes.

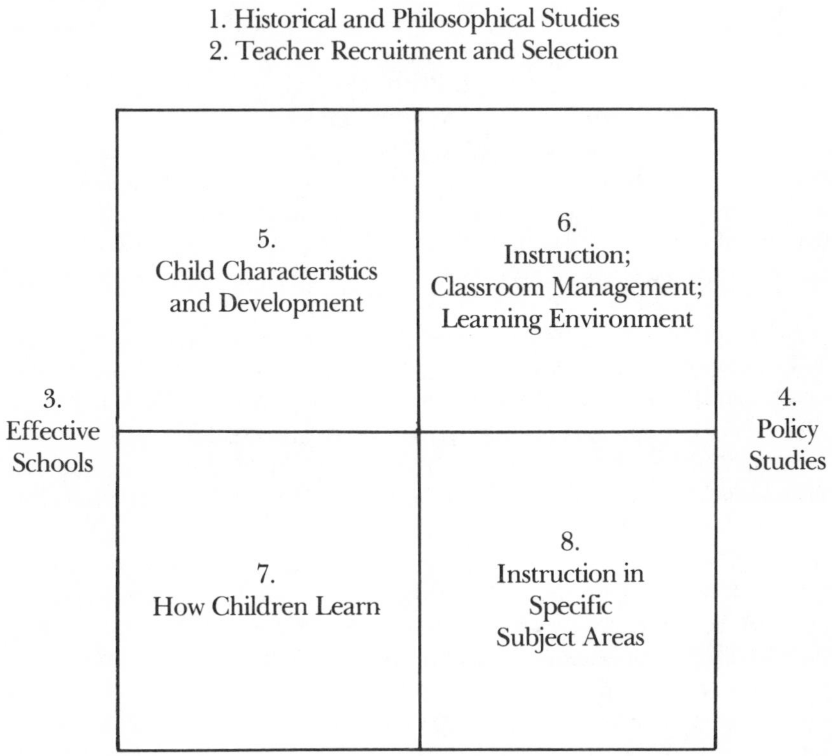

1. Historical and Philosophical Studies
2. Teacher Recruitment and Selection

	5. Child Characteristics and Development	6. Instruction; Classroom Management; Learning Environment	
3. Effective Schools	7. How Children Learn	8. Instruction in Specific Subject Areas	4. Policy Studies

Figure 1. An Eight-Category Structure of Educational Research

Each of the eight sections shown in Figure 1 represents research that is important to education. Some of the sections are more important to prospective teachers; some are more important to educational policy makers; and still others are more pertinent to school administrators.

Historical and philosophical studies are listed first in the sketch because of the overall perspective they provide. The research on teacher recruitment, selection and retention is listed next because unless we succeed in attracting and keeping excellent teachers, all of our talk about excellence in education will go for naught.

School leadership, organization, and climate, as described in the effective schools research (3) have a powerful influence on the way the classroom functions, but they are largely external to the individual classroom, as are the equally influential policies (4) set by legislatures, governors, school boards, and state and federal departments of education.

The box in the middle represents the classroom. It is here that most of what is important in schools takes place. Because the focus of teacher education programs is the teacher in the classroom, the papers in this monograph concentrate on that part of the structure. This is not to deny the importance of the other parts of the diagram; it is simply to recognize the centrality of the teacher—both to schools and to teacher educators.

Within the classroom portion of the diagram, this monograph draws from Section 6 (instruction, classroom management and learning environment), and, to a lesser extent, from Section 5 (child characteristics and development). This is done because the research base is reasonably well developed in these two sections and the research is pertinent to all teachers. For some teacher educators, e.g., reading instructors, a portion of the research in Section 8 (instruction in specific subject areas) would be at least as appropriate as that in Sections 5 and 6, and educational psychologists draw much of the content that they teach from Section 7 (how children learn). (For a more complete description of Sections 6 and 8, see Koehler, 1983.) Information developed through research conducted in Section 6 may be most directly useful to classroom teachers. (See papers by Billups, Stallings, Walter, Vasa, Bruning and Egbert and Kluender, this volume.) Staff members at the Research and Development Center for Teacher Education have used research from Section 6 in the preparation of "how to do it" manuals for elementary (Evertson, et.al, 1984) and secondary (Emmer, et.al., 1984) teachers. Information developed through research conducted in Sections 5 and 7 is more likely to illuminate classroom instruction and management research or to have long-term implications for further research than it is to have immediate utility. (See Santmire and Friesen, this volume.)

Other papers in this monograph consider in some detail six bodies of research. Five of the papers fall rather naturally into Section 6 of the diagram; the remaining paper integrates content from Section 5 and Section 6. It is important to note that the six papers do not represent separate entities; they are all part of what takes place in a classroom and what potential teachers need to know and be able to work with. The content from these papers must be viewed in relation to each other, and that content must be synthesized in teacher education programs.

Discussion

This paper has sketched some ideas about the potential importance of research in education. To provide contrast, education was compared with agriculture. Our research is not as well developed; our mechanisms for transforming research into usable processes and products are not nearly as advanced; and we do not have sufficient commitment to the importance of research information to ensure funding for research and development activities. If leaders in agriculture had been as cavalier in their attitude toward research as we sometimes have been, there would have been no green revolution, there would have been no hybrid corn, and there would have been no dairy surplus. Instead, like the rest of the world, we too would have been living on the margin of our food supply.

This paper also has emphasized the role of teacher education in helping all of education achieve the potential that research holds. As teacher educators, our role is central. We prepare each succeeding generation of teachers, and we provide much of their continuing education.

At this time, several caveats—reservations about this whole task—appear appropriate.

1. There are no drug store pills or fertilizer fixes in education. Maybe someday educational research will turn up something as "clean" as Salk vaccine, but I doubt that *we* will ever see that. In the meantime, we need to use the very best information that we have available from experience and research.

2. Most of the research that educators, or any other professionals, conduct does not produce immediately useful products or processes. In fact, one of the problems with educational research has been that we have not been willing or able to go through the transformation and synthesis essential for making the research useful for practitioners. It is as if the medical profession expected medical doctors to read the chemistry and pharmacology journals and then manufacture their own antibiotics. This is one of the steps that teacher educators must take. We must make appropriate transformations and syntheses of research. This was the initial function of the regional laboratories— to transform research into useful materials and processes and then to disseminate them. Although some of the laboratories have strayed from that mission, others have stayed with it. (See Sikorsky and Ewy, this volume.)

3. The work of changing teacher education programs is not easy. Making substantial changes will require a great deal of both personal and institutional commitment. Work, a willingness to change, a willingness to work together, a willingness to fail and then try again all will be necessary.

References

Bereiter, C., & Kurland, M. (1978, October). *A constructive look at Follow Through results*. Unpublished manuscript, The Ontario Institute for Studies in Education.

Biles, B. L., Billups, L. H., & Veitch, S. C. (1983, April). *Bridging the gap: The AFT educational research and dissemination program*. Paper presented at the annual meeting of the American Educational Research Association, Montreal, Canada.

Billups, L. *The American Federation of Teachers educational research and dissemination program.* (This volume.)

Brophy, J. (1983). Classroom organization and management. *Elementary School Journal, 83,* 265-285.

Bruning, R. H. (1984). Key elements of effective teaching in the direct teaching model. (This volume.)

Darlington, R. (1981). The consortium for longitudinal studies. *Educational Evaluation & Policy Analysis, 3(6),* 37-45.

Denham, C., & Lieberman, A. (1980). *Time to learn.* Washington, DC: National Institute of Education.

Egbert, R., & Kluender, M. (1984). Time as an element in school success. (This volume.)

Emmer, E., Evertson, C., Sanford, J., Clements, B., & Worsham, M. (1984). *Classroom management for secondary teachers.* Englewood Cliffs, NJ: Prentice Hall.

Evertson, C., Emmer, E., Clements, B., Sanford, J., & Worsham, M. (1984). *Classroom management for elementary teachers.* Englewood Cliffs, NJ: Prentice Hall.

Gideonese, H. D. (1983). *In search of more effective service.* USA: S. Rosenthall & Company.

Kilgore, A. M. (1984). Models of teaching and teacher education. (This volume.)

Kluender, M. K., & Egbert, R. L. (1984). *The status of teacher education in the United States.* Accepted for publication. Washington, DC: Clearinghouse on Teacher Education.

Koehler, V. (1983). Introduction: A research base for the content of teacher education. In D. Smith (Ed.), *Essential knowledge for beginning educators.* Washington, DC: Clearinghouse on Teacher Education.

Rosenshine, B. (1983). Teaching functions in instructional programs. *Elementary School Journal, 83,* 335-351.

Santmire, T. E., & Friesen, P. A. (1984). A developmental analysis of research on effective teacher-student interactions: Implications for teacher preparation. (This volume.)

Schweinhart, L. (1983, October). *Quality in early childhood education: The key to long-term effectiveness.* Paper presented at the Kindergarten conference of the Oakland (Michigan) Intermediate School District.

Schweinhart, L., & Weikart, D. (1980). Young children grow up: The effects of the Perry preschool program on youths through age 15. *Monographs of the High/Scope Educational Research Foundation Number Seven.* Ypsilanti, MI.

Sikorski, L., & Ewy. R. (1984). A regional laboratory works with schools. (This volume.)

Smith, B. O. (1983). Closing: Teacher education in transition. In D. Smith (Ed.), *Essential knowledge for beginning educators.* Washington, DC: Clearinghouse on Teacher Education.

Stallings, J. A. (1984). Implications from the research on teaching for teacher preparation. (This volume.)

Stebbins, L., St. Pierre, R., Proper, E., Anderson, R., & Cerva, T. (1977). *Education as experimentation: A planned variation model* (Report No. 76-196A). Cambridge, MA: Abt Associates, Inc.

Time on task. (1982). Arlington, VA: American Association of School Administrators.

Vasa, S. F. (1984). Classroom management: A selected review of the literature. (This volume.)

Walter, L. J. (1984). A synthesis of research findings on teacher planning and decision-making. (This volume.)

On Getting from Here (Research) to There (Practice)*

Gary D Fenstermacher

Virginia Polytechnic and State University

Though it might seem simple, there is no easy way to get from research on teaching to teaching practices. William James said it nearly one hundred years ago:

> You make a great, a very great mistake, if you think that psychology, being the science of the mind's laws, is something from which you can deduce definite programmes and schemes and methods of instruction for immediate schoolroom use (James, 1892, 1958, p. 23).

True enough, modern research on teaching is not like the psychological research at the turn of the century. It typically takes place in school classrooms and is focused on practical problems of teaching. Still, it is research: controlled by prescribed methods, bound by carefully framed questions, and judged on criteria much different from those of the activity of teaching.

It isn't just that research on teaching and actual teaching are different, so you cannot squash the two together. It's also that you should not try to do it. Some people do try to squash them together, and having some limited success at it, declare that it can be done. But they violate countless rules of procedure when they do so (as I have tried to explain elsewhere; see Fenstermacher, 1979). Moreover, trying to make teaching practices directly out of research on teaching has some destructive effects for teaching itself. More on this point later.

If you cannot just leap from research on teaching to good teaching practice, does this mean that the research has no direct implications for teaching practices? No. There is a relationship between the two—a good, healthy relationship, if it is understood and properly used. In the first part of this paper, I will explain the relationship and try to show how it works.

---

*This paper was presented at the Nebraska Consortium for the Improvement of Teacher Education Workshop on November 21, 1983, in Lincoln, Nebraska. Some of the ideas presented here will appear in a chapter on the philosophy of research on teaching, in preparation for the *Third Handbook of Research on Teaching*, edited by Merl C. Wittrock (in preparation).

Practical Arguments

Arguments, like people, come in all shapes and sizes, and forms. Most of the arguments with which we are familiar are in the form of intellectual or theoretical arguments. It is in this form that we debate nuclear disarmament, school attendance policies, or who should wash the dinner dishes. The conclusion to this form of argument is a statement of some kind, such as, "The U.S. should unilaterally reduce its nuclear arsenal," or, "Each member of the family shall take a turn doing the dinner dishes."

Practical argument is a different form. Its conclusion is not a statement of some kind, but an action. A very simple practical argument, adapted from Aristotle's *Nicomachean Ethics*, appears below.

1   Health is a goal I seek
2   Jogging promotes health
3   Early morning is the best time for me to jog
4   It is early morning

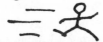

5   _____

There are probably some considerable differences between this practical argument and the arguments to which you are accustomed. One major difference, of course, is the last line in the argument. Note that it is an action, not a statement of some kind. Another difference is that the premises are not linked in the way one would expect, by tight logical conventions and linguistic rules. Yet the argument does seem to hang together, at least at an intuitive level. Consider this argument.

1   Cleanliness is a valued condition of life
2   This office is a mess
3   I have time to clean the office now

4   _____

I apologize for the bizarre stick figures. I hope they are adequate for you to get the point of practical argument. It is the way we reason about many things we undertake in everyday life. They almost always begin with some statement of a goal or desirable state of affairs, proceed through a set of conditions about the world or the situation before us, then acknowledge in some way that the time is right to act, and finally depict an action. These simple examples should convey the general idea. In order to grasp the bearing of practical arguments on teaching research, somewhat more complex examples are in order.

1   Children should learn as much as possible while in school
2   Children in my history class should learn as much history as possible while in my class
3   The most learning occurs when the learner's attention is clearly focused on academic tasks
4   Learning is focused by giving clear instructions, relevant assignments, ample practice, and extensive feedback
5   This is a history class
6   The children are present

7

You cannot tell from the stick drawing that the teacher is doing what premise 4 states needs to be done: "giving clear instructions, relevant assignments, ample practice, and extensive feedback." Why is he doing so? The premise comes from recent research on teacher effectiveness, particularly from the results of the Beginning Teacher Evaluation Study (Denham & Lieberman, 1980; see also Berliner, 1979, and Brophy, 1983). My assumption is that the teacher has become familiar with this research and has incorporated it into a practical argument leading to the actions undertaken in the classroom.

Note that the teacher has adopted as a desirable goal that children learn as much as possible, particularly about history, while in his class. From this goal, the teacher seeks the means for realizing the goal. It is here that research can be extremely beneficial. From relevant research, we gain premises to incorporate into practical arguments governing classroom actions. By linking these research results with goal statements and awareness that the occasion is right for realization of the goal, the teacher engages in actions appropriate to fulfilling the goal.

Research on teaching can be valued for more than *supplying* premises that aid us in finding the means to realize instructional goals. In fact, it is more likely that most teachers come to the classroom already having practical arguments (though perhaps suppressed, or even compressed, as would be the case with maxims such as, "Don't smile until Christmas."). Teachers need help in moving beyond their prior premises.

The educational philosopher, Thomas Green, has worked out the nature of practical argument in the case of the teacher instructing a child. Note what he says, then we will transfer the context to the teaching of teachers.

> The competencies needed by a successful teacher in instruction are those needed to do whatever is required, within moral limits, to (1) change the truth value of the premises in the practical argument in the mind of the child, or to (2) complete those premises, or to (3) add to the range of premises accessible to the child in the formation of practical arguments (Green, 1976, p. 9).

If I understand Green correctly, he is arguing that the teacher tease out the practical argument that undergirds some action or another of the learner, and then work with the child to scrutinize the premises in the argument, for the purpose of (1) changing their truth value, (2) completing ill-formed premises, or (3) supplying additional premises. The same activities may be performed with teachers, for they are learners when first introduced to recent research on teaching.

Note that several premises in the argument about learning in the history class are empirical premises, subject to verification by scientific inquiry. Such premises can be tested, and indeed many have been tested by the research on teaching and schooling. Using the results of this research, it is possible to change the truth values of prior premises (i.e., the evidence from research may show that a given premise, believed by the teacher to be true, is false), or the results may complete heretofore incomplete premises (as when the teacher states she is not sure about this, but "feels" it is the correct procedure), or add to the sophistication and soundness of the argument by supplying additional, empirically grounded premises.

In each case, the argument is changed. As the premises in the argument change, the action following from these premises is also likely to change. It is in this way that research results can be brought to bear on teaching practices—by careful, considered incorporation into the practical arguments in the minds of teachers. It is not an easy procedure, for it requires time, patience, and respect, just as does the teaching of children. Why, then, do it? This question leads us to the second half of the paper.

Manner

Our manner is the way we act over time. We speak of persons being gentle, thoughtful, hateful, compassionate, or just. When we speak like this, we are describing the manner of these persons. Manner refers to traits of character, relatively stable dispositions to act in certain ways given specific circumstances. Thus we say of someone that he has a nice manner, a thoughtful manner, or a considerate manner.

Typically we learn manner by imitating the manner of others, at least at first. We become loving persons because others help us to grasp the value of love and show us how to act in loving ways. We begin to act as they act, because we are trained or encouraged to do so (as in the case of children) or because we choose to be like that (as in the case of older persons). As we practice acting according to a manner, we often adapt it to suit our own personality and circumstances, eventually making it uniquely our own. Then we become models for others, either by setting examples for them because they are young, or by being admired by them and having them choose to be something like us.

Much of what we think of as intellectual and educational virtues are matters of manner (even though we incorrectly identify them as skills; see Passmore, 1975, and Ryle, 1975). Being critical, reflective, deliberative, honest, humble, skeptical, analytical, reasonable, fair, truth-seeking—all these are manners. If the student is to learn them, he must have models.

Persons close to him must exhibit these manners, preferably in relation to the topics that engage student and teacher. If we seek students who are fair, honest, humble, truth-seeking, critical, etc., we must supply them with persons who already possess these manners, these traits of character. Hence, the task is to seek teachers who possess the manner needed to serve as models for the student, or enable teachers to acquire the appropriate manner by training and assisting them.

Each time teachers are taught, those who teach them exhibit manner. If the teacher approves or admires the manner, he or she may imitate it and later adapt it. The special responsibility of teachers of teachers is to possess and exhibit the manner most appropriate to education, to the proper learning of subjects and the acquisition of traits of character which are carefully reasoned and morally justified. Herein lies the reason I have described and explained practical arguments.

By introducing research on teaching to teachers through the analysis and transformation of their practical arguments, we exhibit a manner that shows regard for their prior beliefs and experience, that allows them to engage in their own deliberations about the adequacy of what they are learning and its impact on their actions, and that encourages them to act in the same way as they undertake the teaching of their own students. In other words, the teaching of teachers should serve as a model for how we hope teachers will instruct their students. The concept of practical argument offers a way for us to think about the use of teaching research so that in its presentation to teachers, we can preserve educative ideals, rational sensibilities, and personal autonomy.

I hope I have not sped through all this material at so great a pace that there is no hope you will follow my own intellectual (not practical) argument. If I have not, and have stated my thesis clearly, then you recognize that the idea of practical argument and the concept of manner are intimately linked. This link is a key to thinking how best to teach teachers about research on teaching.

References

Berliner, D. C. (1979). Tempus educare. In Peterson, P. L. & Walberg, H. J. (Eds.), Research on teaching: Concepts, findings, and implications (pp. 120-135). Berkeley, CA: McCutchan Publishing Corp.

Brophy, J. E. (1983). Classroom management and organization. *Elementary School Journal, 83*, 265-285.

Denham, C., & Lieberman, A. (Eds.). (1980). *Time to learn*. Washington, DC: Government Printing Office.

Fenstermacher, G. (1979). A philosophical consideration of recent research on teacher effectiveness. In L. S. Shulman (Ed.), *Review of research in education* (vol. 6). Itaska, IL: F. E. Peacock.

Green, T. F. (1976). Teacher competence as practical rationality. In K. S. Strike (Ed.), *Philosophy of education: 1976*. Urbana, IL: *Educational Theory*, University of Illinois.

James, W. (1958). *Talks to teachers on psychology; and to students on some of life's ideals* (1892). New York: W. W. Norton.

Passmore, J. (1975). On teaching to be critical. In R. F. Dearden, P. H. Hirst, & R. S. Peters (Eds.), *Education and reason: Part III of education and the development of reason* (pp. 25-43). London: Routledge & Kegan Paul.

Ryle, G. (1975). Can virtue be taught? In R. F. Dearden, P. H. Hirst, & R. S. Peters (Eds.), *Education and reason: Part III of education and the development of reason* (pp. 44-77). London: Routledge & Kegan Paul.

A Developmental Analysis of Research on Effective Teacher-Student Interactions: Implications For Teacher Preparation

Toni E. Santmire and Patricia A. Friesen

University of Nebraska-Lincoln

I n 1961, Harvey, Hunt, & Schroder suggested that teachers, parents, and others who function in educational roles with children share at least one common characteristic: they provide an interpersonal environment for the child with whom they interact. Learning takes place within this interpersonal environment. They also suggested that characteristics of that environment could be expected to affect the development of the child. Since that time, research evidence has been accumulating that one important variable in learning or development is the degree of match between relevant characteristics of the learner and those of the environment (Hunt, 1966a; Hunt & Sullivan, 1974; Miller, 1978; 1981).

Hunt (1966b) has taken this argument further to propose that such results have implications for the training of those who provide training environments, e.g., teachers. Using the Lewinian notion that behavior is a function of the interaction between the individual and the environment, he argued that, in order to provide learning environments which would match student characteristics, the teacher would have to understand and be able to identify the relevant characteristics of children and of the environment and then learn to provide an environment matched to student characteristics in ways that would promote desired behavior (Hunt, 1966b; Hunt & Sullivan, 1974).

This is a fairly simple and straightforward argument, and, although presented in an oversimplified form which needs qualification in specific application, it is used both as an overall framework for organizing this review of research on teacher-student interactions as they affect teaching effectiveness and as a basis for developing the implications of this research for teacher education.

A major reason for taking this approach is not inherent in the approach itself, but is inherent in the nature of developmental psychology as a discipline. Developmental psychology is the study of changes that occur across the life span. To say that children change is a truism. Teachers know that kindergarten students are different from second graders, are different from

28

fifth graders, are different from eighth graders, are different from high school sophomores, are different from high school seniors. Teachers also know that children need to be treated differently from adolescents; that they need to have a different learning environment.

If we take seriously the research on matching and the idea that the differences in children and adolescents will determine the nature of the characteristics of the environment which will result in optimum learning and/or development, then we need to understand the nature of the differences between various ages/stages in development and how they may affect what children or adolescents will respond to in the environment. Such understanding has been enhanced by recent research and theory in developmental psychology which has provided a reasonably good description of the nature of important changes which occur during the school years and how these changes relate to some salient characteristics of children's and adolescents' perceptions of and response to various aspects of their environment.

Although both the nature of developmental change and the characteristics of effective teachers have been active areas of research over the past decade, they have rarely informed each other in ways suggested by the above argument. In what follows, a synthesis of these two areas is attempted. Such a synthesis will provide a basis for understanding why given teacher characteristics or behaviors are effective at one grade level and not at another. This understanding can then be used to analyze and inform the content of teacher preparation programs.

Developmental Changes
During the School Years

An important basis for understanding the nature of the developmental changes across the school years has been provided by the work of Piaget and his colleagues in the area of the developmental characteristics of thinking (e.g., Inhelder & Piaget, 1955/1958; Inhelder & Piaget, 1964/1969). Other investigators have found parallel stages in areas of social development including a) relations with adults and peers (Youniss, 1980), b) understanding of the perspectives of others (Feffer, 1959; Feffer & Gourevitch, 1960; Flavell, 1977; Flavell, Botkin, Fry, Wright, & Jarvis, 1968; Selman & Jaquette, 1977), c) moral reasoning (Kohlberg, 1969), d) understanding of social conventions (Furth, 1980; Turiel, 1977), e) religion (Elkind, 1961, 1962a, 1963; Elkind & Elkind, 1962; Fowler, 1981), and f) personality development including the development of a sense of personal identity (Erikson, 1959/1980, 1963, 1968) and the concept of self (Broughton, 1978; Elkind, 1981).

The discussion of development which follows attempts to integrate these sources to develop as comprehensive a picture as possible (in the limited space available) of the expectable cognitive and social characteristics of children and adolescents as they change across the school years.

It is possible to understand many of the characteristic behaviors of children of different ages by making the assumption that children use an underlying mode of thought which undergoes developmental change to understand the world around them. The descriptions of developmental changes in cognitive, personality and social development over the school years appear to be consistent with the notion that the underlying mode of thought changes from a mode that is based on the image in preschool and elementary school to one based on concepts represented by language in junior high and high school.

The image was discussed by Piaget (1945/1951) as developing out of the sensorimotor thought of infancy and being intermediate between that type of thinking and the conceptual thought of the adult. The image is probably best understood as being something like a photograph. While children's images undoubtedly include elements other than visual (e.g., auditory, tactile, kinesthetic), they appear to share with the photograph the characteristic of being a *direct* representation of children's experience of particular situations/people/events. That is, they are "pictures" in children's minds, and have the status of being a direct representation of the actual and specific situation as experienced by the child.

Unlike images, signs (including language) are not direct representations of actual situations. Instead, they have an arbitrary relationship to what they represent in the sense that the pattern of sounds utilized to represent a concept does not inhere in the concept in the way that the structure or pattern of colors in a photograph inheres in a particular picture. For example, the sound pattern used to designate one's female parent could as easily be "angmar" as "mother." This arbitrariness of language eventually allows thought to break away from the "concrete" image to become "abstract."

There are two major changes in the underlying mode of thought across the school years. In the preschool period the image is the primary mode of thought. Furthermore, thought uses images that are constructed in the context of *immediately present experience*. During this period, language is involved in thinking only as it is or has been incorporated into children's experiential images.

Sometime between the ages of five and seven a change begins to occur and, while the image remains the underlying mode of thought, *language becomes able to construct images in the absence of immediately present experience*. Development of the ability to construct images from language is consolidated during the elementary school years. This consolidation generally consists of children abstracting, more and more precisely, the meaning of the concepts of the language. They do this by figuring out how concepts relate to other concepts in describing images. For example, preschool children use the term grandfather in the presence of a specific person or of people who have similar physical characteristics, whether or not they are actually grandfathers. On the other hand, nine or ten-year-olds understand that their grandfather is the father of their father or mother and that everyone has grandfathers. They understand that not all older men are grandfathers. They can, therefore, use the word grandfather to create an image of a specific person, for example in a story, and one of the aspects of that image is that the character is the father of one of the parents of the children in the story.

Once this consolidation is stable it leads to the recognition that more than one set of concepts could be used in a given situation and that the different sets would give rise to different images. For example, there are other conceptual systems than those of family relations which could be used to describe the storybook grandfather. He might be president of a corporation, a doctor, or a policeman. The search to reconcile the various ways of classifying leads to the second major change in mode of thought, the development of abstract thinking in adolescence.

Because each development undergoes a period of transition and then a period of consolidation, the school years from kindergarten through twelfth grade encompass five identifiable periods. For convenience and ease of identification, the Piagetian labels for these periods will be used in this paper. Late Preoperational Thought defines the period in which the image is still primary; it is characteristic of preschool children. Early and Late Concrete Operational Thought will be used for the period in which the image is becoming organized by the concepts of the language, and Early and Late Formal Operational Thought for the period in which thought is freed from the specific image.

It is important to include a discussion of all of these stages because, while stages can be identified by age/grade level for many children, development is never as clear-cut in real life as it appears in this sort of description. Growth is very much a product of experience. In areas where children have had considerable experience of the right nature, they may exhibit behavior which is characteristic of children older than their own age. In areas where experience is limited, development might lag behind that of children of comparable age (Uzgiris & Hunt, 1975). This means that a given child might exhibit behavior that is characteristic of more than one "stage" at any given age. It also means that not all children of the same age will be at the same "stage" in any given area of experience.

The majority of children in the elementary school years fall into the stages of early and late concrete operations with the transition between them occurring somewhere between third and fourth grade. A significant number of kindergarten children use late preoperational reasoning and some first and even second grade children may be preoperational in some areas of thinking. On the other end of the elementary school age spectrum, as many as ten percent of sixth-grade children have started the transition into adolescence and exhibit characteristics of early formal operations. Increasing numbers of students become early formal operational during the junior high school years. By the junior year of high school, the characteristics of late formal operational thought appear in some students.

While it appears that almost everyone but severely mentally retarded individuals becomes concrete operational, this is not the case with formal operational thinking. Various studies show that a significant proportion of adults do not show the characteristics of formal operations in some areas of development. The percentages vary with the population studied, the area of development being investigated, and the stringency of the criteria used, and range from 20% to 70% of the study sample showing formal operations (c.f., Kuhn, Langer, Kohlberg, & Haan, 1977; Neimark, 1975; Rowe & Marcia, 1980). Amount of education is clearly associated with the development of formal operational reasoning, although it is not so clear in which direction the causal relationship lies (Neimark, 1975). It is, however, apparent that a number of adults are not yet at the level of late formal operational thought. The significance of this for teacher-student interaction will be discussed later in the paper.

Developmental
Characteristics and Effective Teaching

The nature of the changes discussed above may be expected to have dramatic effects on the nature of the teacher-student interactions which will promote effective teaching. The research on effective teacher-student interactions rarely directly addresses the question of the developmental changes or of the match between environmental characteristics and those of the child, although the research on Aptitude-Treatment-Interaction (ATI) provides some evidence in this regard (Miller, 1981). For the most part, the research examines teacher behavior as input and student learning or attitude as outcome without regard for the effect of any matching that might occur. While some authors (e.g., Brophy, 1983) recognize that there are differences in students in different grades (he calls these context variables) which will call for different teaching practices, such differences have generally not been systematically studied in this literature.

For the purposes of synthesizing the developmental psychology and teacher effectiveness literature, research and theory from developmental psychology has been summarized from the perspective of the hypothesized underlying modes of thought for each of the five stages which are found in school-age children and adolescents. The research on characteristics of effective teaching was summarized by grade level, selecting for analysis those characteristics which have either appeared at one grade level and not at others or which differed from one grade level to another. Then an attempt was made to relate what works or does not work at each level to the characteristics of children of that level which had been derived from the developmental analysis. From this analysis some fairly consistent patterns emerged which can be related to developmental characteristics of students. Where possible, these patterns have been grouped into two general and somewhat arbitrary clusters: a) teacher-student instructional interactions, and b) characteristics of teacher control/management strategies. Some research on effective teaching in adolescent populations has been reviewed which specifically examines the match between developmental and environmental characteristics as a variable.

Late Preoperational Thought
(Preschool and Kindergarten)

Thinking at this stage is dominated by the internal image of immediately present experience. Present images are related to past images through perceptual similarities, but the two seem to merge into one image (Piaget, 1945/1951). At this stage children have good command of the adult language of the home, but that language is simply a part of the image for them rather than separate from it. Consequently, language can be used to describe an image or to direct attention to salient features of an image. Piaget (Inhelder & Piaget, 1964/1969) speaks of children of this age as being perception bound. He also describes the thought of the preoperational child as analogous to a series of "still" images much like the individual frames of a movie film (Piaget, 1945/1951).

Progression to the next stage is presumed to result from increased facility in describing images by language. This increase is apparently due to increases in descriptive vocabulary, accuracy in understanding the meaning of words, and in grammatical complexity. These increases are presumed to occur as children attempt to communicate about their images.

The primacy of the image of immediate experience of this stage is consistent with research results in various areas of preschool behavior. Because preoperational children are tied to what is immediately in front of them, they have difficulty coordinating information from one image to another. This results in their failure to be able to perform on the Piagetian conservation tasks. They are unable to coordinate information from one part of the problem (one image) with that from another (a second image) because their image changes with the shift in attention (Piaget, 1941/1965). Similarly, preoperational children have difficulty seriating or classifying objects consistently. In these tasks they tend to either form perceptual wholes (e.g., build houses or trains) or to shift the basis they are using to classify or seriate from one object to the next. Olver and Hornsby (1966) labeled this phenomenon "edge-matching." The coordination of past with present in the image leads to the distorted time sense of children of this age (Elkind, 1981).

Because images are direct representations of reality, they can only be described literally. Metaphoric language is interpreted literally (Gardner, Kircher, Winner & Perkins, 1975). The image is a "positive" representation of experience. It represents experience, not its "negative." For this reason, preoperational children have a difficult time inhibiting actions when the direction is "Don't do . . . " (Luria, 1961). Another characteristic of preoperational children which is consistent with the view that they are bound to images of immediate experience is their inability to distinguish appropriate from inappropriate behavior, and winning at games from losing at them. Kohlberg (1969) has shown that the criteria used by children of this age for evaluating behavior in moral dilemma situations are based on which acts are punished and which are not. Piaget (1932/1962) showed that children of this age did not use consistent criteria for deciding whether someone had won a game, nor were they able to coordinate the specific actions which go into a game into a regular sequence.

Perhaps the flavor of preoperational thinking is best captured by an example. These abound in A. A. Milne's *Winnie-the-Pooh*:

> Once upon a time, a very long time ago now, about last Friday, Winnie-the-Pooh lived in a forest all by himself under the name of Sanders.
>
> ("What does 'under the name' mean?" asked Christopher Robin.
>
> "It means he had the name over the door in gold letters and lived under it . . .") (Milne, 1926, p. 3).

In this passage are examples of the assimilation of everything that happened previously to being long past and of the nature of the preoperational image of what it means to "live under the name of . . . "

Viewing the thought of preoperational children in this way allows the derivation of some implications for educational environments. Preoperational children may be expected to have difficulty in meeting some classroom expectations that older children understand more readily. Preoperational children may be expected to have problems when expectations require images which are not readily available, for example, a) when the environment is unfamiliar, b) when instructions are to carry out actions which are new, c) when the instructions describe actions in an abstract rather than literal way (e.g., "Clean up the room," as opposed to "Put your pencils in your desk."), d) when there is more than one instruction in a string, or e) when the instruction is to not do something. Children need to be shown specifically what to do and each demonstration should be accompanied by a verbal description with children then doing and describing for themselves. Demonstrations and carrying out of such instructions should be repeated in context until children can carry them out alone. Instructions should not be expected to generalize to new situations because images are situation specific. Demonstrations should be repeated as children need them.

The same sort of considerations apply to instruction of content. Central attention should be given to the coordination of descriptive language with the activity of the child. Instruction not tied to physical activity of children or to children's spontaneous questions may be expected to be less effective.

While there is relatively little research specifically on characteristics of effective teaching in kindergarten, some studies of both kindergarten and first and second grades have yielded results which are in line with these expectations. From the perspective of behavior management, a technique which has been found to be helpful to children through second grade in learning to control their own behavior is a modeling with verbalization procedures. At first, students watch the instructor model the desired behavior while describing the actions verbally. Then the students are helped to talk through the behavior as they do it themselves (Camp & Bash, 1981; Meichenbaum & Goodman, 1971). This technique has been used largely with children who are behavior problems in the classroom and it has been criticized because it does not appear to be reliably successful above the second- or third-grade level (Brophy, 1983) and because the behavior learned fails to generalize beyond the specific situation in which it is utilized (Pressley, 1979).

From a developmental perspective, this technique can be seen as reliably associating language with image, a skill which is supposed to be occurring during the late preoperational period and which will lead to progression to the next stage. Thus, it makes developmental sense to use this sort of teaching technique at this stage. To the extent that children who are behavior problems in first and second grades lag developmentally behind their peers, this technique should prove helpful. Its failure to generalize is to be expected developmentally. The image of preoperational children is so situation specific that children may not see the similarity unless it is verbally called to their attention. It should not be expected to work as well at later stages because older children may be expected to misbehave for reasons other than lack of behavioral understanding of verbal commands or the lack of an "appropriate image" for the situation.

Amount of teacher talk is negatively correlated with reading achievement for low socioeconomic status (LSES) first- and second-grade students (Soar, 1973). Deutsch (1973) reports that LSES children are apt to have a lower mean level of cognitive development than middle class children. Preoperational children need to be actively relating words to experience/images. Teacher talk, unless carefully and consistently related to children's activity, may be expected to confuse more than teach in the preoperational period. Once children are concrete operational, however, this should be less true because words assist in constructing images in the later period.

From the perspective being developed here, later learning will depend, at least in part, on the coordination of image and language laid down in the late preoperational stage. As children become better and better able to use language to describe the images of thought, they become better and better able to use language to create reliable images in the absence of the real situation. A major reason for the provision of a kindergarten experience at the end of this stage is to help children learn the image base for many of the concepts and appropriate student behaviors which they will need in later schooling. Children's learning such words as larger, older, right, left, three, etc., as they describe their perceptions of immediate situations is facilitated by their being provided with a situation and having their actions in that context talked about in the same terms over and over again. This facilitates the consolidation of the connection between image and related language.

Once children are able to evoke the same image reliably through the use of the same words, they gradually become able to create images in their minds and to compare these images with one another. It is this ability to create and compare images which is presumed to underly movement to the next stage (Piaget & Inhelder, 1966/1969).

Early Concrete Operations (Grades 1 to 3)

In all of the concrete operational period it appears that the image is still the underlying mode of thinking. The difference between concrete operations and preoperations is the *ability to use adult language to accurately construct images in the absence of immediately present experience*. This ability appears to allow children to hold more than one image in mind at one time, which, in turn, allows comparison of images of past and present, enabling children to begin to understand what remains constant and what changes as one image is transformed into another. This allows the formation of true concepts, that is, ideas which represent the common or constant aspects of objects as opposed to their particular manifestation in a given image. In early concrete operations, children begin to abstract the meanings of concepts out of their images. This is a gradual process which becomes increasingly consolidated over the period.

A body of developmental research is available which is consistent with this view of the nature of thought in concrete operations and which also sheds further light on its nature. Piaget's work on conservation, classification and seriation (cf., Piaget, 1941/1965; Inhelder & Piaget, 1964/1969) shows that children at this stage can coordinate information in ways which allow them to build systems of concepts and relationships. Early concrete operational children appear to be limited, however, in that they can only use one "constant" or relationship at a time.

Weir (1964) reports, for example, that children of this age are poor problem solvers, tending to perseverate on an initial point of view even when it appears to be contradicted by evidence (from the adult perspective). Their verbalizations indicate that they find a way to reconcile the evidence with their point of view rather than *vice versa*. Peel (1960) reports similar data.

The research on role-taking is also consistent with the conception of early concrete operational thinking as being limited to a single concept or relation at a time. Children of this stage use their own conception of what to do in a situation and do not coordinate it with the view of others of the same situation (Flavell et al., 1968; Selman & Jaquette, 1977). When asked to retell stories from the perspective of different characters, children simply retell the same story (Feffer, 1959; Feffer & Gourevitch, 1960).

The focus on a simple basis for understanding an event helps to explain why children do not coordinate their understanding that they have to pay for goods with an understanding that shopkeepers also have to pay for the goods they sell. It is as if, in one event, they buy and the shopkeeper sells; but the shopkeeper does not buy (Furth, 1980). Children of this stage view social conventions as simple descriptions of regularities in social behavior (Turiel, 1977).

The ability to abstract information to form true concepts enables children to begin to have an understanding of what it means to win at games (e.g., have more marbles than the other), but they still do not have a conception of all of the rules and how they fit together to regulate the game. They consistently "modify" the rules (to their advantage) and they eliminate from the game any rules that are in dispute (Piaget, 1932/1962). Consistent with this, their criteria for evaluation of behavior as good or bad center around a "naive hedonism" in which that behavior is good which serves to meet one's needs (Kohlberg, 1969).

Implications of this view of early concrete operations for educational environments can be derived for both management of instructional processes and classroom behavior. Instructionally, it would appear that lessons should be focused on a single concept or operation, should involve direct instruction, and then give the children the opportunity to practice using the concept or relation in a variety of contexts. Because the children's own images are being used to abstract the concepts, such images should be evoked through involving children in active response or through active interaction with illustrative materials. This latter should be particularly important where the children's background has not provided immediate experience from which the concepts being taught can be readily abstracted.

Characteristics of effective teaching at this level are supportive of these expectations. The most effective instructional interactions in these grades are strongly teacher directed. Teacher initiated interactions characterized by low-level (on Bloom's taxonomy) or product questions are positively correlated with achievement; inquiry or inferential, high-level questions are negatively correlated with achievement in these grades (Brophy & Evertson, 1974, 1976; Coker, Lorentz, & Coker, 1976; Soar, 1973; Stallings & Kaskowitz, 1974). The effective teacher calls on each student in a systematic way to respond or practice a skill, and does not rely on volunteers (Brophy & Evertson, 1974). Whether students are working in large groups or individually, it is important that the teacher monitor work closely (Anderson, Evertson, & Emmer, 1980; Berliner & Tikunoff, 1976; Brophy & Evertson, 1976; McDonald & Elias, 1976; Soar, 1973). Reading scores increase when teachers respond with paraphrases or rephrases of student comments (Good, Biddle, & Brophy, 1975; Martin, Veldman, & Anderson, 1980), and classroom work related to student interests and background is more effective (Emmer, Evertson, & Anderson, 1980).

All of these techniques are consistent with early concrete operational children's need to learn to organize their images using adult concepts. Low-level questions with immediate correction through rephrasing and practice are essential to consolidation of these concepts. Because there are many potential concepts which could be used, children need teacher direction to focus on what is important. Inquiry and discovery techniques can allow students the freedom to focus on relationships which are not important in organizing conceptual systems for academic work.

Children are presumed to be constructing the concepts important to schooling during this stage. Consequently, they should not be expected to be able to know when their work is correct. This is consistent with research indicating that children of this age view effort, rather than ability or knowledge, as the important element in success (Frieze & Snyder, 1980; Nicholls, 1978).

In the management of social behavior in the classroom, it is important to remember that, although children can construct an image of the goals of activity and means of attaining those goals, they have no conception of the appropriateness of those means. Clear standards of what is appropriate and inappropriate need to be established and consistently maintained. Children need to be shown how to do the appropriate things, over and over again, in order to abstract out the constancy in various situations from the image.

Consistent with this, it appears that students at this age level are best served by teachers who teach students how to behave through direct instruction and sequential practice in appropriate behaviors such as getting materials, putting them away, getting a drink and cooperating with classmates (Anderson et al, 1980). Effective teachers do not ignore inappropriate behavior; they act quickly to stop disruptive behavior through additional instruction in appropriate behavior rather than prohibition and punishment (Anderson et al., 1980; Coker et al., 1976; Emmer et al., 1980).

Late Concrete Operations (Grades 4-6)

According to the perspective on thinking being developed in this paper, in late concrete operations, the underlying mode of thinking is still the image constructed by language. The primary difference between early and late concrete operations appears to be that children in the latter stage begin to coordinate the relations constructed in early concrete operation with each other. For example, Piaget reports that late concrete operational children can form multiple classifications and seriations and they have a clearly differentiated conception of the concepts of "some" and "all" (Inhelder & Piaget, 1964/1969). They begin to coordinate temporal sequences between events into cause-effect relationships (Inhelder & Piaget, 1955/1958).

A new skill also appears. Children begin to be able to understand content outside their own experience by applying the concepts abstracted from that experience to the new content (Inhelder & Piaget, 1955/1958; Inhelder & Piaget, 1964/1969). This looks like hypothetical thinking in the sense that children are making predictions about unknowns, however, they still use primarily descriptive concepts and are unable to coordinate these concepts in a logical way.

For example, late concrete operational children are able to describe what happens to the trajectory of a billiard ball as the angle of the cue is changed, and this allows them to make predictions about new trajectories based on past experience. They do not, however, examine the logical relationship of reciprocal implication as a way of understanding possible relationships between angle of incidence and angle of reflection, and so do not arrive at the law of equality (Inhelder & Piaget, 1955/1958).

In social interactions, late concrete operational children begin to coordinate their own perspective of what is important in a situation with the consequences of the fact that they assume that the other person in the interaction will share their perspective on what is important. They then adjust their behavior based on that assumption (Flavell et al., 1968; Selman & Jaquette, 1977). They understand that different characters in a story may perceive the same event from a different point of view, and adjust their telling of the story accordingly (Feffer & Gourevitch, 1960).

Children at this stage have complete and detailed knowledge of rules of games and how they interrelate to regulate interindividual perspectives in games (Piaget, 1932/1962). They understand that shopkeepers buy what they sell to customers (Furth, 1980) and that social conventions are arbitrary (Turiel, 1977). Consistent with these orientations are the criteria which children of this stage use to determine good and bad. Actions are good if they are consistent with what is approved by others, the so-called "good boy" orientation (Kohlberg, 1969).

Students with these capabilities may be expected to present a somewhat different problem for instructional and behavioral management than that posed by children of earlier stages. Assuming that they have good knowledge of important concepts, children of this stage should benefit from instruction in which relevant conceptual systems are juxtaposed and the implications of that juxtaposition explored. They should also benefit from the systematic use of existing concepts to understand new content, for example, the use of addition and subtraction in teaching multiplication and division. These activities need to be strongly teacher directed at the outset because children have no criteria to decide which are academically important concepts and which are unimportant.

These expectations are consistent with data that indicate that instructional interactions involving a moderate frequency of low-level questioning and increased frequency of pupil initiated interaction and discussion promote achievement in a variety of subject areas (Coker et al., 1976; Gall, 1977; Good & Grouws, 1977; Taebel & Coker, 1980). Because students lack internal criteria for knowing the correct conceptual system to use, it is important for teachers to help students understand what to do by being clear and avoiding ambiguity (Beck, 1967; Good & Grouws, 1977; Samuels & Griffore, 1980). When students have difficulty, process explanations are effective (Good & Grouws, 1977). Teacher clarity improves performance on higher level questions (Winne, 1977).

In the area of social behavior, children recognize the arbitrariness of standards for appropriate behavior and are oriented toward doing what is approved. This has the potential of leading to some seriously inappropriate behavior through the mechanism of peer influence because that which is peer approved is as valid as that which is adult approved. On the other hand, there is a repertoire of appropriate behavior built up from prior experience. There may be less need for direct instruction in appropriate behavior than earlier, however, consistent maintenance of standards and monitoring of potential trouble is necessary.

These characteristics imply that classroom management will be a somewhat different problem than earlier. Now, generally appropriate behaviors should not be viewed as routines to be taught, but as conduct to be expected. Insistence on attention to task and conformity appears to facilitate achievement as does acting quickly to stop disruptive behavior (Good & Grouws,

1977; Good et al., 1975). On the other hand, because students do not want to stand out, overt teacher praise is less effective in this age group than earlier (Brophy, Rohrkemper, Raschid, & Goldberger, 1983; Good & Grouws, 1977; Samuels & Griffore, 1980). Now children start to distinguish skill from effort as variables in success and more difficult tasks are more rewarding (Nicholls, 1978). Thus, effective teachers focus on task involvement (Good & Grouws, 1977), and do not distract students or raise anxiety levels by reminding students about their work or threatening them with time limits (Brophy, 1983).

Early Formal Operations (Grades 7-10)

Piaget observed that, somewhere around the age of twelve, the logical reasoning, which he labeled formal operations, begins. This reasoning is characterized as focusing on the possible ways of conceptualizing a situation rather than focusing on the description of images of reality, as in earlier stages (Inhelder & Piaget, 1955/1958). It is consistent with this change in orientation to suggest that the underlying mode of thinking has shifted from the image to the conceptual systems which have come to represent the image during concrete operations. This, in essence, is consistent with the conceptualization of the second signal system of Vygotsky (1934/1962).

As with earlier stages, data exists which is consistent with the notion that thought becomes freed from the image in this stage. Piaget's data suggest that early adolescents utilize alternative conceptual systems to analyze situations although they are not yet able to use logic to coordinate these conceptual systems into the set of all possible combinations. Consequently, they develop some hypotheses in a somewhat unsystematic fashion, test these against reality (i.e., experiment), and use the data and additional hypotheses suggested by the experiment to develop a system which is consistent with the data. This period, then, can be seen as a stage of moving back and forth between the image generated by the experiment and constructions generated by purely conceptual analysis.

Similar characteristics are observed in social areas. By the end of the late concrete operational period, children have moved from recognizing the arbitrary nature of the behavioral regularities which are supposed to govern interpersonal relations to a basic respect for general rules of interpersonal conduct (Turiel, 1977). Harvey, Hunt, and Schroder (1961) identify this behavior as Stage I in their system of personality development. Kohlberg (1969) found this orientation in his fourth stage, the "law and order" stage of the development of moral reasoning. This coordination of concrete behavioral regularities into one overarching system marks the consolidation of concrete operational thought.

In the early formal operational period, changes in these systems appear, all of which suggest a freeing of thought from the specific concrete action and a recognition that more than one rule system can apply to a given situation. Turiel (1977) reports that twelve- to thirteen-year-old adolescents begin to view the rules that they simply accepted earlier as being arbitrary. Harvey, Hunt, and Schroder (1961) find that individuals begin to recognize that rules need to be modified to take individual circumstances into account. Kohlberg (1969) finds that individuals begin to move toward an orientation which regards morality in terms of a social contract which coordinates alternative systems of internal principles of conduct. Elkind (1981) suggests that adolescent idealism is probably a function of the adolescent's ability to construct a hypothetically ideal world in comparison with which the real world comes up wanting.

Feffer (1970) reports work which finds that adolescents do not simply recognize that different characters in a story have different perspectives on events, they begin to construct elaborated characters whose independent characteristics yield the different perspectives.

This view of early adolescent thinking suggests that, at this age, youth can be expected to be able to generate alternatives to almost any specific action or set of concepts used to deal with any given situation. It also implies that, unless these ideas are tested against reality, they may be seen as having validity equal to that of any other point of view. This has two implications for educational environments. Where the alternatives can be tested for empirical validity, adolescents need to have the opportunity to develop and make the tests, preferably on their own. Secondly, when, as is often the case, the criteria for evaluating the alternatives arise out of different value systems, adolescents need to be exposed to the value implications of the alternatives because they will not see them on their own.

Early adolescents do not have the criteria to judge what constitutes an adequate answer to a problem because they do not yet see it as a whole. Thus they need adults to keep that in front of them. Instructional environments, consequently, need to focus on setting up situations or circumstances where adolescents can either generate and defend their own point of view based on factual evidence or develop and defend alternatives to existing points of view. Frequently, this is fruitfully done through peer interaction in humanities and social science coursework. In the natural sciences, it can be done through a combination of course and laboratory work if the labs are not simply repetition of someone else's work. Labs need to be designed to answer questions which have been raised in the minds of students. Instruction needs to be oriented toward developing these questions and helping students generate answers and test them against the facts.

Data on effective teaching in the junior high grades is hard to find and more difficult to interpret. One possible reason for this is that students are no longer in self-contained classrooms and there is the possibility that what constitutes effective teaching in one discipline is somewhat different than what constitutes effective teaching in another (Evertson, Anderson, & Brophy, 1978). There is also some difficulty in assessing achievement other than specific knowledge of math and science (Evertson & Emmer, 1982). A third difficulty may stem from the developmental heterogeneity of the typical junior high school classroom.

Nevertheless, a consistent finding is that student initiated interactions and analytic and inquiry oriented questions continue to increase in importance. Students of this age make better use of teacher explanations than earlier, and teachers who incorporate student ideas into their teaching are better liked or judged to be more clear (Coker et al., 1976; Evertson et al., 1978; Evertson & Emmer, 1982; Evertson & Veldman, 1981; Flanders, 1965; Fraser & Fisher, 1982; Kennedy, Cruickshank, Bush, & Meyers, 1978). On the other hand, the availability of alternative possibilities without internal criteria for decision making may be expected to make students insecure in their own knowledge. Thus, math teachers who asked questions of volunteers were more effective on achievement measures and students in English classes had strongly negative attitudes if teachers called on nonvolunteers (Evertson et al., 1978).

Management of classroom behavior can also be expected to be a problem with early adolescents. They become unwilling to respond unquestioningly to authority. This is because they can generate their own alternatives and do not yet understand the criteria used for making choices. Thus they test rules, both because they regard rules as arbitrary and because they have an experimental attitude; they want to see what happens when they do something contrary to the rules.

Adolescents need the opportunity to test and question, to be treated as adults but also to be helped to control their own behavior by discussing it beforehand (if possible) or afterward in a way which is nonjudgmental. This is a disorganized period for adolescents, and minor transgressions need to either be ignored or treated lightly in a way which reminds students of expectations and the reasons for them. On the other hand, early adolescents need to have firm expectations and not be let get out of control. Serious problems need to be dealt with immediately, but not in a way that makes the adolescent defensive. Prevention by limiting alternatives may be expected to be effective as may discussion in terms of reasons for expectations and consideration of individual circumstances.

Classroom management techniques which appear to be differentially effective with junior high students include dealing with students' feelings, both positive and negative, teacher confidence, establishing a spirit of cooperation between student and teacher and joking with students (Chiapetta & Collette, 1980; Flanders, 1965; Moskowitz & Hayman, 1976). On the other hand, being one of the group, socializing with students, or being a showman was not correlated with effectiveness, at least in math teachers (Evertson et al., 1978; Flanders, 1965). Effective classroom managers ignore minor misbehavior but intervene rapidly to prevent discipline problems using consistent control techniques (Evertson et al., 1978; Evertson & Emmer, 1982).

Late Formal Operations (Grades 11 and beyond)

In late formal operations thought appears to become totally free of the image in the sense that the interrelations among concepts used become manipulable based on their conceptual interrelationships rather than their relations within the specific image. In the case of the logical operations described by Piaget, the descriptive conceptual systems which apply to the problem at

42

hand are interrelated logically prior to experimental test rather than concomitant with it. Critical tests which eliminate rival hypotheses for explaining the interrelationships are also conceptualized and systematically carried out (Inhelder & Piaget, 1955/1958).

In the area of social behavior, characteristics appear which seem to be similar to this sort of hypothesis generation and testing. Actions are evaluated as good or bad on the basis of internalized principles of conduct based on universal human rights (Kohlberg, 1969). Individuals enter a "moratorium" status in which they explore different identities, that is, different hypotheses about central values and commitments (Erikson, 1959/1980, 1968; Marcia, 1980; Rowe & Marcia, 1980). They now regard social conventions as a means of regulating social interactions which embody the shared values of the particular group in which they exist (Turiel, 1977). Harvey, Hunt, and Schroder (1961) find that individuals in this stage are exploring themselves in relation to the culture in the process of integrating a coherent self-system which is differentiated from the cultural "personality."

Individuals at this stage may be expected to be beyond the point of questioning for the sake of questioning. They look at new information in relation to what they already know, determine if it fits their existing hypothesis about what is operating in a given situation, and modify their thought or action accordingly. Individuals in this stage search for new knowledge in purposeful and directed ways. The search is based on whether or not they can fit new facts into existing frameworks. These individuals begin to fit knowledge together into disciplines and to think like mature adults. They learn what they want to learn, think for themselves, and can begin to make up their own minds about what they think about a given subject. They may be expected to become selective, deciding for themselves what is important.

These students may be expected to present quite different problems in terms of instructional and behavioral management than students of earlier ages. Because they recognize the need for social conventions appropriate to the specific group, they can be expected to be basically conforming to any rational set of expectations. They may, however, become quite activist about expectations which seem discriminatory or to be an infringement of their rights. The main problem in instructional management will be motivational. These individuals will not be motivated to pursue subjects which are not of interest to them. In large part, what they may be expected to see as of interest depends upon the breadth of prior education. The broader prior training has been, the more interrelated knowledge will become in this period. Instruction which emphasizes this interrelationship will be of more appeal.

Research on effective teacher-student interactions which can be used to test these expectations is almost nonexistent at this level. This is particularly true when achievement is used as the measure of effectiveness. High school students do, however, give high ratings to teachers who respect their opinions (Bowman, 1960 in Samuels & Griffore, 1980; Palonsky, 1977). A significant source of difference in opinion between high school students and teachers in some schools, but not others, is that over the degree to which students should have a voice in academic decisions (Marsh, 1979; Smith & LaPlante, 1980).

Research on Student-Environment Interaction in Adolescence

As was noted above, there are relatively few studies on effective teaching practices in this age range. One potential reason for this is that there are a variety of developmental levels in any age-graded group above sixth grade. By senior high school, developmental divergence is apparent both within and across programs. In general populations almost 30% of sophomores are formal operational (Shayer, Kuchemann, & Wylam, 1976). A correlation with ability is apparent in the fact that in high ability groups, up to 86% of the students are formal operational (Shayer & Wylam, 1978). The correlation is, however, far from perfect. In one study, seniors in college-prep classes had a few students in early concrete operations (4%), and the most students in formal operations (73%). In contrast, vocational students were 23% early concrete operational and 4% formal operational (Chiapetta & Whitfield, 1977). If, in fact, developmental status is related to the characteristics of effective instruction, then studies of teaching in developmentally heterogeneous groups might show inconsistent effects. Initially, Evertson et al. (1978) were puzzled by the inconsistent pattern of significant results produced by their data from junior high English classrooms. Having found their observational data on teacher effects in math classes to be stable (Evertson, Anderson, Edgar, Minter, & Brophy, 1977; Emmer, Evertson, & Brophy, 1979) they then reanalyzed the English data in terms of the effects of degree of heterogeneity (by student ability) on student engagement (Evertson, Sanford, & Emmer, 1981). Higher heterogeneity in junior high English classes was associated with less student task engagement and cooperation and less successful teacher adaptation of instructional materials.

A group of researchers in the area of personality development has recognized the problem of heterogeneity among junior high and high school students and conducted research in this age range which attempts to look at the interaction between developmental status and environmental characteristics. Although only a few of their studies are classroom observation studies, their results are suggestive enough that they need to be included here.

The research in question arises out of Conceptual Systems Theory (Harvey et al., 1961) which provides a theoretical framework explicitly suggesting that characteristics of the individual interact with characteristics of the environment to produce behavioral outcomes. The theory suggests that individuals develop through a sequence of stages starting from a position of reliance on external standards and definition of right and wrong at the onset of adolescence through a period of self definition to a position of interdependent relations with the environment. In most individuals this development occurs at different rates and, as with formal operations, adult populations show a wide range of developmental levels (Harvey, White, Prather, Alter, & Hoffmeister, 1966).

The theory states that individuals will prefer interpersonal environments which are matched to the interpersonal expectations that accompany a particular position in the developmental sequence. They will also learn more in such environments.

Students in secondary school range between the early stage and middle stage of conceptual level (CL) development with all levels present in all grades from seven through twelve. In general, there are developmental effects on learning, with students at more advanced developmental stages achieving at higher levels. This is particularly pronounced when achievement is assessed by measures involving more advanced processes on Bloom's taxonomy (Hunt, Joyce, Greenwood, Noy, Reid, & Weil, 1974; McLachlan & Hunt, 1973; Noy & Hunt, 1972; Tomlinson & Hunt, 1971; Zampogna, 1975).

The nature of preferred environment and that which produces higher achievement also varies with developmental status. In general, students at earlier stages of the developmental sequence prefer and/or achieve best in instructional modes where they are told what they are to learn first and then presented with supporting material (Tomlinson & Hunt, 1971) and where independent study is minimized (Tuchman & Orefice, 1973, Zampogna, 1975) as in some lectures (McLachlan & Hunt, 1973). They tend to follow rules established for the inductive process rigidly and to the letter rather than using them as guidelines, as do students at later stages (Hunt et al., 1974).

In contrast, students at middle stages in the developmental sequence tend to achieve better in and to prefer learning environments where there is less direct teaching (McLachlan & Hunt, 1973; Tomlinson & Hunt, 1971, Zampogna, 1975).

A few studies have specifically found matching effects in which students achieve better in environments which are matched to their developmental level and worse where there are mismatches (Hill, 1969; Santmire, 1969).

The results of this research are consistent with those derived from the teacher effectiveness studies, and provide good support for it. Because of the developmental complexity of secondary school groups, this latter type of research appears more fruitful for investigating teaching effectiveness than the more typical process-product design.

Thus, early in this particular developmental sequence individuals should prefer and learn best in highly structured environments in which the instructor is the authority figure who sets standards, directs learning and maintains discipline. At intermediate levels, individuals should prefer and learn best in environments which encourage self expression, self-directed learning and opportunity for comparisons of alternative viewpoints. Authoritarian environments are resisted. At later levels individuals should prefer environments in which they can both contribute and benefit, although they can probably learn well in any environment that provides specific information they feel relevant to their needs. Junior high and high school students can be expected to be in early and early middle stages.

Research to test the validity of these expectations has been conducted both experimentally and naturalistically in junior high, senior high, and some higher educational settings (Miller, 1981). Both achievement and preference for types of instruction have been dependent measures.

The research reviewed in this section provides empirical validation for something we all know intuitively. Students at different ages are different and need to be treated differently in the provision of instructional environments in which they can learn effectively. What is of more importance, however, is that these differences appear to be systematic differences related to the nature of the cognitive and social developmental status of the children. This relationship means that developmental psychology can be used as a theoretical framework for understanding how some effects of teaching occur. This should enable us to more systematically create effective learning environments in schools.

Implications for Teacher Preparation

The synthesis of developmental psychology and teacher effectiveness research which has been attempted here has two sets of implications for teacher preparation. One set of implications is for the content of the program, the other is for the instructional interactions through which teacher preparation is achieved.

In terms of program content, it is apparent that Hunt's (1966b) argument that teachers need to be able to identify relevant student characteristics, decide what environmental characteristics are appropriate, and have the skill to set up an environment which provides them, should be taken seriously. Based on theory and research reviewed above, some specific recommendations can be made.

1. Teacher trainees need to develop a conceptual understanding of the nature of the developmental changes that occur in children generally across the school years and in detail in the grade level range they are preparing to teach.

2. The data suggest that age is not a good indicator of developmental status, although it is better at the elementary school level than at the secondary school level. This means that prospective teachers must be trained to assess developmental status using the student behaviors which are characteristic of the various stages and of various areas of development.

3. Teacher trainees need to be trained to modulate what they expect of and do with children, based on their assessment of their developmental status. The teacher effectiveness literature reviewed above has specific suggestions which can be used as starting points.

4. If the relationship between developmental status, behavioral characteristics, and effective teaching practice can be communicated, teacher trainees may be able to use their knowledge of developmental psychology to determine what to do when specific techniques that they have learned do not apply.

The second set of implications of this body of research is more unusual, but equally important. We cannot ignore the developmental status or our own students in planning our programs!

46

All of the studies which have assessed developmental status of college students and adults, in either cognitive or personality domains, have found a wide range of developmental levels (e.g., Elkind, 1962b; Hunt & Joyce, 1967; Kuhn et al., 1977; Murphy & Brown, 1970; Rowe & Marcia, 1980). Students range from late concrete operational to equilibrated formal operational and from early to middle levels of personality development.

Again, some specific recommendations can be made based on the research reviewed above.

1. The inclusion of some form of practicum experience is very important. For the more concrete students, it will provide an image base for the concepts we are trying to teach—providing that we use descriptive concepts at first. For the more abstract students, it will provide a testing ground for the development and testing of hypotheses related to effective teaching—providing we help them to develop and test those hypotheses.

2. Our classes need to be organized to meet the developmental needs of our students. More concrete students need low-level concepts presented in clear, unambiguous contexts, without distracting complications, at least until these concepts are well learned. Discussion of issues will be frustrating, although discussion of examples and extensions of conceptual systems should prove interesting and challenging. More abstract students will want opportunities to express their ideas about issues, and may benefit more from inquiry oriented techniques within the context of the cognitive content.

The specific recommendations outlined above are only a few of those that might be developed given the research available. At least as important, however, is the integration of the two bodies of research. This integration allows an understanding of why specific teacher-student interactions work or do not work at different stages of development. This should enable the development and testing of still further techniques. That is, rather than looking only at what has been done that has been effective in the past, we should now be able to suggest new techniques that might be expected to work on a proactive basis.

The integration of these two bodies of knowledge should also be fruitful for developmental psychology. It does not simply confirm some developmental theory, it confirms the usefulness in the "real world" of some of its concepts. It may provide a model for conducting at least some research which integrates basic and applied research, in ways which lead to new understanding.

References

Anderson, L. M., Evertson, C. M., & Emmer, E. T. (1980). Dimensions in classroom management derived from recent research. *Journal of Curriculum Studies, 12,* 343-356.

Beck, W. R. (1967). Pupils' perceptions of teacher merit: A factor analysis of five postulated dimensions. *The Journal of Educational Research, 61*, 127-128.

Berliner, D. C., & Tikunoff, W. J. (1976). The California Beginning Teacher Evaluation Study: Overview of the ethnographic study. *Journal of Teacher Education, 27*, 24-30.

Brophy, J. E. (1983). Classroom organization and management. *The Elementary School Journal, 83*, 265-285.

Brophy, J. E., & Evertson, C. M. (1974). *Process-product correlations in the Texas Teacher Effectiveness Study: Final Report.* Austin: University of Texas.

Brophy, J. E., & Evertson, C. M. (1976). *Learning from teaching: A developmental perspective.* Boston: Allyn & Bacon.

Brophy, J., Rohrkemper, M. Rashid, H., & Goldberger, M. (1983). Relationships between teachers' presentations of classroom tasks and students' engagement in those tasks. *Journal of Educational Psychology, 75*, 544-552.

Broughton, J. (1978). Development of concepts of self, mind, reality, and knowledge. *New Directions for Child Development, 1*, 75-100.

Camp, B. W., & Bash, M. A. (1981). *Think aloud: Increasing social and cognitive skills--a problem-solving program for children (primary level).* Champaign, IL: Research Press.

Chiappetta, E. L., & Collette, A. T. (1980). Identification of science teacher competencies for implementing ISIS minicourse instruction. *Science Education, 64*, 53-58.

Chiappetta, E. L., & Whitfield, T. D. (1977) An examination of cognitive development among academically tracked high school seniors. *The High School Journal, 61*, 31-37.

Coker, H., Lorentz, J. L., & Coker, J. G. (1976). *Interim report on Carroll County CBTC Project, Fall, 1976.* Georgia State Dept. of Education.

Deutsch, C. P. (1973). Social class and child development. In B. M. Caldwell & H. N. Ricciuti (Eds.), *Review of child development research* (Vol. 3, pp. 233-282). Chicago: University of Chicago Press.

Elkind, D. (1961). The child's conception of his religious denomination: I. The Jewish child. *Journal of Genetic Psychology, 99*, 209-225.

Elkind, D. (1962a). The child's conception of his religious denomination: II. The Catholic child. *Journal of Genetic Psychology, 101*, 185-193.

Elkind, D. (1962b). Quantity conceptions in college students. *Journal of Social Psychology, 57*, 459-465.

Elkind, D. (1963). The child's conception of his religious denomination: III. The Protestant child. *Journal of Genetic Psychology, 103*, 291-304.

Elkind, D. (1981). *Children and adolescents: Interpretive essays on Jean Piaget* (3rd ed.). New York: Oxford University Press.

Elkind, D., & Elkind, S. (1962). Varieties of religious experience in young adolescence. *Journal for the Scientific Study of Religion, 2*, 102-112.

Emmer, E. T., Evertson, C. M., & Anderson, L. M. (1980). Effective classroom management at the beginning of the school year. *The Elementary School Journal, 80,* 219-231.

Emmer, E. T., Evertson, C. M., & Brophy, J. E. (1979). Stability of teacher effects in junior high classrooms. *American Educational Research Journal, 16,* 71-75.

Erickson, E. B. (1963). *Childhood and society* (2nd ed.). New York: Norton.

Erikson, E. H. (1968). *Identity: Youth and crisis.* New York: W. W. Norton.

Erikson, E. H. (1980). *Identity and the life cycle.* New York: W. W. Norton (Original work published 1959).

Evertson, C. M., Anderson, L. M., & Brophy, J. E. (1978). *Texas junior high school study: Final report of process-outcome relationships* (Report No. 4061). Austin: University of Texas, Research and Development Center for Teacher Education. (ERIC Document Reproduction Service No. ED 173 744)

Evertson, C., Anderson, L., Edgar, D., Minter, M., & Brophy, J. (1977). *Investigation of stability in junior high school math and English classes: The Texas Junior High Study* (Report Series No. 4051). Austin: University of Texas, Research and Development Center for Teacher Education. (ERIC Document Reproduction Service No. ED 143 692)

Evertson, C. M., & Emmer, E. T. (1982). Effective management at the beginning of the school year in junior high classes. *Journal of Educational Psychology, 74,* 485-498.

Evertson, C. M., Sanford, J. P., & Emmer, E. T. (1981). Effects of class heterogeneity in junior high school. *American Educational Research Journal, 18,* 219-232.

Evertson, C. M., & Veldman, D. J. (1981). Changes over time in process measures of classroom behavior. *Journal of Educational Psychology, 73,* 156-163.

Feffer, M. H. (1959). The cognitive implications of role-taking behavior. *Journal of Personality, 27,* 152-168.

Feffer, M. (1970). A developmental analysis of interpersonal behavior. *Psychological Review, 77,* 197-214.

Feffer, M. H., & Gourevitch, V. (1960). Cognitive aspects of role-taking in children. *Journal of Personality, 28,* 383-396.

Flanders, N. A. (1965). *Teacher influence, pupil attitudes, and achievement.* Washington, DC: U.S. Department of Health, Education, and Welfare.

Flavell, J. H. (1977). The development of knowledge about visual perception. In C. B. Keasey (Ed.), *Nebraska Symposium on Motivation* (pp. 43-76). Lincoln: University of Nebraska Press.

Flavell, J. H., Botkin, P. T., Fry, C. L., Wright, J. W., & Jarvis, P. E. (1968). *The development of role-taking and communication skills in children.* New York: John Wiley & Sons.

Fowler, J. W. (1981). *Stages of faith: The psychology of human development and the quest for meaning.* San Francisco: Harper & Row.

Fraser, B. J., & Fisher, D. L. (1982). Predicting students' outcomes from their perceptions of classroom psychosocial environment. *American Educational Research Journal, 19,* 498-518.

Frieze, I. H., & Snyder, H. N. (1980). Children's beliefs about the causes of success and failure in school settings. *Journal of Educational Psychology, 72,* 186-196.

Furth, H. G. (1980). *The world of grown-ups: Children's conceptions of society.* New York: Elsevier.

Gall, M. D. (1977). The importance of context variables in research on teaching skills. *Journal of Teacher Education, 28(3),* 43-48.

Gardner, H., Kircher, M., Winner, E., & Perkins, D. (1975). Children's metaphoric productions and preferences. *Journal of Child Language, 2,* 125-141.

Good, T. L., Biddle, B. J., & Brophy, J. E. (1975). *Teachers make a difference.* New York: Holt, Rinehart & Winston.

Good, T. L., & Grouws, D. A. (1977). Teaching effects: A process-product study in fourth-grade mathematics classrooms. *Journal of Teacher Education, 28(3),* 49-54.

Harvey, O. J., Hunt, D. E., & Schroder, H. M. (1961). *Conceptual systems and personality organization.* New York: Wiley.

Harvey, O. J., White, B. J., Prather, M. S., Alter, R. D., & Hoffmeister, J. K., (1966). Teachers' belief systems and preschool atmospheres. *Journal of Educational Psychology, 57,* 373-381.

Hill, L. E. (1969). A study of levels of conceptual functioning and their relationship to student achievement and student perception of teachers. Unpublished doctoral dissertation, Syracuse University.

Hunt, D. E. (1966a). A conceptual systems change model and its application to education. In O. J. Harvey (Ed.), *Experience, structure and adaptability.* New York: Springer.

Hunt, D. E. (1966b). A model for analyzing the training of training agents. *Merrill Palmer Quarterly, 12,* 137-155.

Hunt, D. E., & Joyce, B. R. (1967). Teacher trainee personality and initial teaching style. *American Educational Research Journal, 4,* 253-259.

Hunt, D. E., Joyce, B. R., Greenwood, J., Noy, J. E., Reid, R. M., & Weil, M. (1974). Student conceptual level and models of teaching: Theoretical and empirical coordination of two models. *Interchange, 5,* 19-30.

Hunt, D. E., & Sullivan, E. V. (1974). *Between psychology and education.* Hinsdale, IL: Dryden.

Inhelder, B., & Piaget, J. (1958). *The growth of logical thinking: From childhood to adolescence.* New York: Basic Books. (Original work published 1955).

Inhelder, B., & Piaget, J. (1969). *The early growth of logic in the child.* New York: Norton (Original work published 1964).

Kennedy, J. J., Cruickshank, D. R., Bush, A .J., & Meyers, B. (1978). Additional investigations into the nature of teacher clarity. *Journal of Educational Research, 72,* 3-10.

Kohlberg, L. (1969). Stage and sequence: The cognitive-developmental approach to socialization. In D. A. Goslin (Ed.), *Handbook of socialization theory and research* (pp. 375-404). New York: Rand McNally.

Kuhn, D., Langer, J., Kohlberg, L., & Haan, N. S. (1977). The development of formal operations in logical and moral judgment. *Genetic Psychology Monographs, 95*, 97-188.

Luria, A. R. (1961). *The role of speech in the regulation of normal and ab- normal behaviors.* London: Pergamon.

Marcia, J. E. (1980). Identity in adolescence. In J. Adelson (Ed.) *Handbook of adolescent psychology* (pp. 159-187). New York: Wiley.

Marsh, C. J. (1979). Teachers and students don't agree about what should go on in high schools. *The High School Journal, 63*, 67-71.

Martin, J., Veldman, D. J., & Anderson, L. M. (1980). Within-class relationships between student achievement and teacher behaviors. *American Educational Research Journal, 17*, 479-490.

McDonald, F. J., & Elias, P. (1976). *The effects of teaching performance on pupil learning. Beginning teacher evaluation study: Phase II, 1973-1974* (Final Report: Vol. 1). Princeton, NJ: Educational Testing Service.

McLachlan, J. F., & Hunt, D. E. (1973). Differential effects of discovery learning as a function of student Conceptual Level. *Canadian Journal of Behavioral Science, 5*, 152-160.

Meichenbaum, D., & Goodman, J. (1971). Training impulsive children to talk to themselves. *Journal of Abnormal Psychology, 77*, 115-126.

Miller, A. (1978). Conceptual systems theory: A critical review. *Genetic Psychology Monographs, 97*, 77-126.

Miller, A. (1981). Conceptual matching models and interactional research in education. *Review of Educational Research, 51*, 33-84.

Milne, A. A. (1926). *Winnie-the-Pooh.* New York: Dutton.

Moskowitz, G., & Hayman, J. L. (1976). Success strategies of inner-city teachers: A year-long study. *The Journal of Educational Research, 69*, 283-289.

Murphy, P. D., & Brown, M. M. (1970). Conceptual systems and teaching styles. *American Educational Research Journal, 7*, 529-540.

Neimark, E. D. (1975). Intellectual development during adolescence. In F. D. Horowitz (Ed.) *Review of child development research.* (Vol. 4, pp. 541-594). Chicago: University of Chicago Press.

Nicholls, J. G. (1978). The development of the concepts of effort and ability, perception of academic attainment, and the understanding that difficult tasks require more ability. *Child Development, 49*, 800-814.

Noy, J. E., & Hunt, D. E. (1972). Student-directed learning from biographical information systems. *Canadian Journal of Behavioral Science, 4*, 54-63.

Olver, R. R., & Hornsby, J. R. (1966). On equivalence. In J. S. Bruner, R. R. Olver, & P. M. Greenfield (Eds.), *Studies in cognitive growth* (pp. 68-85). New York: Wiley.

Palonsky, S. B. (1977). Teacher effectiveness in secondary schools: An ethnographic approach. *The High School Journal, 61*, 45-51.

Peel, E. A. (1960). *The pupil's thinking.* London: Oldhourne.

Piaget, J. (1951). *Play, dreams and imitation in childhood.* New York: Norton (Original work published 1945).

Piaget, J. (1962). *The moral judgment of the child.* New York: Collier (Original work published 1932).

Piaget, J. (1965). *The child's conception of number.* New York: Norton (Original work published 1941).

Piaget, J., & Inhelder, B. (1969). *The psychology of the child.* New York: Basic Books. (Original work published 1966).

Pressley, M. (1979). Increasing children's self-control through cognitive interventions. *Review of Educational Research, 49,* 319-370.

Rowe, I., & Marcia, J. E. (1980). Ego identity status, formal operations, and moral development. *Journal of Youth and Adolescence, 9,* 87-99.

Samuels, D. D., & Griffore, R. J. (1980). Students' perceptions of the characteristics of "good teachers. *Journal of Instructional Psychology, 7,* 28-34.

Santmire, T. E. (1969). *An investigation of the role of student conceptual level and teacher-radiated environment in achievement.* Unpublished doctoral dissertation, University of Rochester.

Selman, R. L., & Jaquette, D. (1977). Stability and oscillation in interpersonal awareness: A clinical-developmental analysis. In C. B. Keasey (Ed.), *Nebraska Symposium on Motivation* (pp. 261-304). Lincoln: University of Nebraska Press.

Shayer, M., Kuchemann, D. E. & Wylam, H. (1976). The distribution of Piagetian stages of thinking in British middle and secondary school children. *British Journal of Educational Psychology, 46,* 164-173.

Shayer, M., & Wylam, H. (1978). The distribution of Piagetian stages of thinking in British middle and secondary school children. II - 14 to 16-year-olds and sex differentials. *British Journal of Educational Psychology, 48,* 62-70.

Smith, J. K., & LaPlante, D. A. (1980). Student and teacher perceptions of fair versus unfair teacher activities and the problem of teacher legitimacy. *The High School Journal, 64,* 108-114.

Soar, R. S. (1973). *Follow through classroom process measurement and pupil growth (1970-1971)* (Final report). Gainesville, FL: University of Florida, College of Education.

Stallings, J., & Kaskowitz, D. (1974). *Follow through classroom observation evaluation 1972-1973. A study of implementation.* Menlo Park, CA: Stanford Research Institute.

Taebel, D. K., & Coker, J. G. (1980). Teaching effectiveness in elementary classroom music: Relationships among competency measures, pupil product measures, and certain attribute variables. *Journal of Research in Music Education, 28,* 250-264.

Tomlinson, P. D., & Hunt, D. E. (1971). Differential effects of rule-example order as a function of learner Conceptual Level. *Canadian Journal of Behavioral Science, 3,* 237-245.

Tuchman, B. W., & Orefice, D. S. (1973). Personality structure instructional outcomes, and instructional preferences. *Interchange, 4,* 43-48.

Turiel, E. (1977). Social convention and morality: Two distinct conceptual and developmental systems. In C. B. Keasey (Ed.) *Nebraska Symposium on Motivation* (Vol. 25, pp. 77-116). Lincoln, Nebraska: University of Nebraska Press.

Uzgiris, U. C., & Hunt, J. McV. (1975). *Assessment in infancy: Ordinal scales of psychological development.* Urbana, Illinois: University of Illinois Press.

Vygotsky, L. S. (1962). *Thought and language.* Cambridge: MIT Press (Original work published 1934).

Weir, M. W. (1964). Developmental changes in problem solving strategies. *Psychological Review, 71,* 473-490.

Winne, P. H. (1977). Aptitude-treatment interactions in an experiment on teacher effectiveness. *American Educational Research Journal, 14,* 389-409.

Youniss, J. (1980). *Parents and peers in social development.* Chicago: University of Chicago Press.

Zampogna, J. A. (1975). *A study of the relationship between learning styles and learning environments in selected secondary modern foreign language classes.* Unpublished doctoral dissertation, State University of New York at Buffalo.

A Synthesis of Research Findings on Teacher Planning And Decision Making

L. James Walter

University of Nebraska-Lincoln

Students preparing to teach receive abundant information regarding the need for planning. They are taught multiple planning models and they review examples of lesson plans for both long-range and daily use. Most often the approaches they are taught follow a rationale refined by Ralph Tyler (1949) over thirty years ago. This approach advocates deriving student objectives from several sources: the learners' needs and interests, the subject matter or formal disciplines, and societal needs. Because there are potentially more objectives than educators have resources to implement, choices must be made. Tyler suggests using (1) what is known about psychology of learning, and (2) philosophical beliefs about education as "screens" to limit the number of objectives which educators seek to implement. Based upon that delimitation, decisions about specific classroom objectives, selection of learning activities, organization of activities and evaluation of student outcomes would be made by individual teachers. This model is often referred to as the "ends-means" model because of the emphasis on identification of objectives (in terms of student outcomes) before considering the activities for students or "means" of instruction.

The Tyler Model has had a pervasive impact on teacher education. A review of current methods books indicates that several chapters in each book are devoted to planning using the "ends-means" approach. For instance, Henson (1983) devotes three chapters to planning and divides the task into long-range and short-range planning. Both planning foci begin with "objective" setting followed by decisions about "materials" and "learning activities." The "selection of a topic" is the initial step listed in Callahan and Clark (1977). This is followed by "selection of general and specific objectives." Determining the learning activities is the fourth step listed. Kim and Kellough (1983) begin with the "determination of objectives" followed by the "development of learning experiences for students." In their methods book Armstrong and Savage (1983) suggest that teachers should "diagnose student needs before" selecting content and "objectives."

Despite the emphasis given in teacher education to the "ends-means" approach, there now exists much evidence which indicates that experienced teachers don't begin the planning process by determining objectives. Most researchers conclude that teachers begin the planning process by determining the content to be covered and then design or select learning activities for students (Zahorik, 1975; Walter, 1979; Shavelson & Stern, 1981).

With the emphasis given in methods texts and courses to an "ends-means" approach to planning, why don't teachers follow this systematic, behavioral model? Simple explanations may suggest that teachers need more time for planning, fewer preparations or improved instructional resources, but before one can describe reasons teachers make the decisions they do, more should be known about the decision-making processes teachers use. The remainder of this paper provides an overview of research on teacher decision making with attention given to decisions teachers make before they teach and decisions they make while they are engaged in interactive teaching.

Clark and Joyce (1981) developed a model for studying the types of decisions which teachers make. They used Hunt's Model, which was designed to construct a network of teaching decisions, to organize and interpret data from their study. They grouped decisions into: (1) selecting and clarifying objectives; (2) identifying components of learning styles; (3) selecting appropriate learning environments; and (4) initiating, maintaining and adapting learning environments. The categories were considered to be a beginning in developing a comprehensive taxonomy of teacher decision making which considers the multitude of variables teachers encounter in executing their responsibilities.

To better understand the processes of decision making that teachers use, Shavelson and Stern (1981) considered how humans, in general, process information. They concluded that (1) persons' abilities to process information from their environments are limited, and (2) people tend to process information in a sequential, step-by-step fashion.

> As a consequence of these information processing limitations, people selectively perceive and interpret portions of available information with respect to their goals, and construct a simplified model of reality. Using certain heuristics, attributions and other psychological mechanisms, people then make judgments and decisions and carry them out on the basis of their psychological model of reality (Shavelson and Stern, 1981, p. 461).

As a reference to guide the understanding of research on teacher planning and decision making, Clark and Joyce (1981) suggested that answers to four questions are in order. (1) What are teachers' thoughts as they are planning to teach? (2) What thinking behaviors are present while teachers are teaching? (3) What are the behavior patterns teachers manifest during interactive teaching? and (4) What do students learn as a result of the transactions (listed in 1-3)?

Planning Decisions Before Teaching

Teachers participate in planning for teaching at a variety of levels. They serve on district-level curriculum committees to assist with the planning of formal curricula. Additionally, they do individual long-range planning, usually at the beginning of the school year, for classes they are assigned to teach (Shavelson 1981). This long-range plan includes decisions about students as well as activities, goals, major projects and general requirements for the year. Units of study, which may take several weeks to complete, are planned during the course of school year as are weekly plans, such as those found in teacher planning books. Of course teachers do daily planning, too. Inexperienced teachers do far more daily planning than those who are experienced.

District-level involvement by teachers is well documented. Such participation is generally viewed as critical for successful curriculum change to take place, although too frequently, teachers are asked to do curriculum work after teaching a full day in the classroom. Determining the appropriate amount of teacher involvement in curriculum planning is dependent upon many variables. Schaffarzik (1976) concluded that school districts use a wide variety of models to make curriculum decisions and both teacher and citizen participation has increased in recent years; however, he also reported that their involvement may be somewhat superficial with major decisions still being made by higher authorities. He urged better mechanisms and forums for teacher and citizen participation. Tibbetts (1979) reported on the consequences when teachers lose decision-making power and are required to blindly adhere to prescribed programs imposed from outside. She concluded that this loss of autonomy leads to decline in teachers' interest with a consequent loss to the students.

Saylor (1982) outlined the major influences on teachers in a model he entitled, "The Curriculum Plans Reservoir." In that comprehensive model, he defined curriculum as "a plan for providing sets of learning opportunities for persons to be educated" (p. 2). He stated that it is the teacher "who is guiding and directing the organized learning activities of students in a school setting as the ultimate curriculum planner" (p. 2). As the teacher carries out this complex task, a number of significant and powerful groups and agencies influence the types of decisions that teachers make. Saylor described external and internal agencies who formulate guidelines as two categories of major influences on teachers. Figure 1 illustrates these agencies and shows roles played by federal and state government. The chapters in the Saylor reference outline the contributions made by each agency and the nature of their influence. The "curriculum reservoir" is drawn upon by the teacher for guidance and help and, in some instances provides mandated programs which must be followed.

Figure 1 - THE CURRICULUM PLANS RESERVOIR

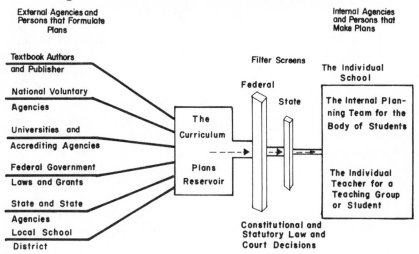

External Agencies and
Persons that Formulate
Plans

Internal Agencies
and Persons that
Make Plans

Textbook Authors
and Publisher

National Voluntary
Agencies

Universities and
Accrediting Agencies

Federal Government
Laws and Grants

State and State
Agencies

Local School
District

The
Curriculum

Plans
Reservoir

Filter Screens

Federal

State

Constitutional and
Statutory Law and
Court Decisions

The Individual
School

The Internal Plan-
ning Team for the
Body of Students

The Individual
Teacher for a
Teaching Group
or Student

From Saylor, 1982, p. 3

The long-range planning that teachers do early in the school year has a profound impact on their decisions for the remainder of the year. Teachers make decisions about content, activities, groupings of students, major projects, grading schemes and rules for student behavior in these early plans. Shavelson and Stern (1981) pointed out that, unless researchers carefully examine planning which teachers do early in the year, important aspects of the decision-making process will be missed. Marx (1981) also concluded that the number of decisions which teachers make decrease as units they are teaching progress. From this research, it appears that the number of decisions and the impact of those decisions tends to diminish as the school year progresses.

Considering information about students is most prevalent in decisions made early in the year. Shavelson and Stern (1981) reported that during the early part of the school year teachers are "getting to know" their students and once teachers reached a judgment, less attention is given to students while planning. Most attention to students' needs was focused on a group of students with little attention paid to individuals within the group or their needs (Clark & Peterson, 1976; Shavelson & Stern, 1981).

Research studies on short-range decisions which teachers make before teaching specific lessons have used a technique called process tracing (Shavelson & Stern, 1981). Teachers are asked to "think out loud" into a tape recorder while planning lessons or solving an instructional problem. Clark and Joyce (1981), in describing findings of several authors who used such techniques, concluded that few teachers, without formalized training, establish objectives before teaching. Instead they rely on instructional materials for selection of method, content and learning activities. Shavelson and Stern (1981) reported that teachers begin planning by identifying tasks or instructional treatments for students. These tasks are developed into instructional activities which serve as the unit of planning and action in the classroom.

To avoid confusion, a learning activity will be referred to as an instructional task—a building block in the curriculum. Tasks consist of several elements (see Figure 2). *Content* is one of the most important elements and teachers consider the textbook as the major (and usually only) source of content. A second element is the *materials* used to teach the task. The *activity*, the third element, consists of the things teachers and students will do in the task. *Goals* are a fourth element. These are not stated behaviorally but are general statements of student outcomes. A fifth element is the *student*. Consideration is for the group of students (Shavelson & Stern, 1981). Teachers use these tasks as mental images or "scripts" to guide their behaviors during interactive teaching.

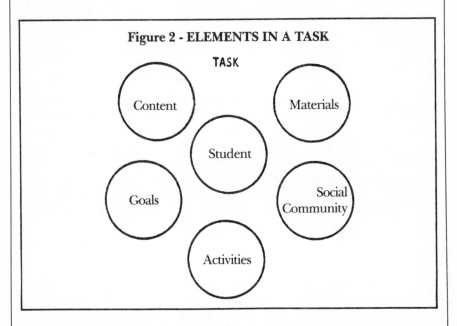

Figure 2 - ELEMENTS IN A TASK

From Shavelson and Stern, 1981, p. 478
Copyright 1981 American Educational Research Association, Washington, DC

Most research on teacher planning abilities has been descriptive. It has focused on exposing differences between theoretical planning models and the practical experience of teachers. McNergney and others (1983) have developed a process to assess teachers' planning skills. The assessment tool is variation of the "in basket" technique developed to assess administrative abilities to make planning decisions. Using a multiple choice format, the researchers designed an instrument to assess teachers' abilities to apply professional knowledge. Such a tool has great potential for teacher educators as they work with teachers to improve planning abilities.

Teacher Decisions While Teaching

Decisions which teachers make while they are teaching are referred to as *interactive decisions*. Measuring these "on their feet" decisions is usually done using a process called stimulated recall. Clark and Peterson (1976) used this process to determine what teachers thought about while teaching.

Conceptualizing teaching as clinical information processing, Clark and Peterson viewed the teacher as the information processor. The model that they developed centered on the teacher's ability to observe changes in student behavior and make judgments about the changes which were occurring.

Clark and Peterson hypothesized that teachers would use information gained by reading student cues to make decisions changing their teaching performances. The study was conducted to gain information on the correspondence between their model and how teachers processed information while teaching. They studied twelve experienced teachers in a laboratory setting teaching social studies lessons to groups of eight junior high students. After the lessons were taught, the researchers used a stimulated recall technique to gain insight into teachers' thought processes while teaching. Teachers were shown video tapes of the lessons and asked a series of six questions. The questions were designed to elicit information in correspondence with the model the researchers had constructed.

Based on the results of the study, Clark and Peterson concluded that: (1) teachers considered alternative plans only when the instructional process was going poorly; (2) the involvement of the students and student participation were the principal cues teachers used to determine the adequacy of the instructional process; and (3) teachers rarely changed their plans, even when the instructional was going poorly. Joyce and Brown (1981) also have concluded that teachers change their routines only when things are going exceedingly bad.

In their landmark review of research on teacher decision making, Shavelson and Stern (1981), as noted above, developed a model of teachers' decision making during interactive teaching (see Figure 3). In developing the model they concluded that the instructional tasks serve as "scripts" for carrying out interactive teaching. Teachers are primarily concerned with maintaining a constant flow of activity to prevent classroom management problems. They concluded, as did Clark and Peterson (1976), that teachers are very reluctant to change from their tasks or routines. To consider changing routines increases the information processing load for teachers and increases the probabilities for classroom management problems. Teachers seem to make few decisions to change their teaching behavior during interactive teaching (Clark & Peterson, 1976). It is estimated that teachers make between 9 and 13 decisions per hour of instruction. When they do change, few alternatives are considered before a decision is made (Shavelson and Stern, 1981).

Figure 3 - MODEL OF TEACHERS' DECISION MAKING DURING INTERACTIVE TEACHING

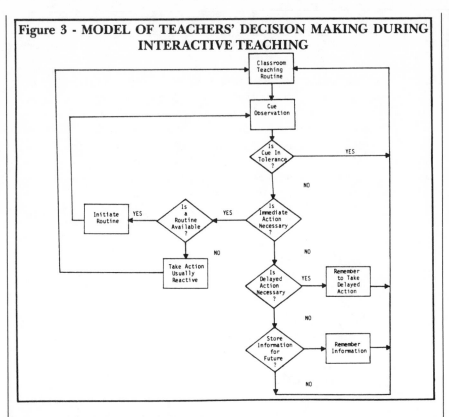

From Shavelson and Stern, 1981, p. 483

Whether, as teachers gain experience, they become more skilled in handling the information processing load and making decisions during interactive teaching, was the focus of research conducted by Fogarty, Wang and Creek (1983). Their study focused on the student performance cues which led to teachers' implementation of instructional action, the instructional actions employed, and instructional goals and other information teachers considered during the instructional process. Using three experienced elementary teachers (average of 10.1 years of experience) and five inexperienced interns, the researchers used stimulated recall to collect data on "decision points" which the researchers had identified in each teaching episode. They also developed a system to classify the student performance cues and the instructional actions teachers used.

Fogarty et al. concluded that differences between experienced and novice teachers were apparent and centered on the failure of the novices to implement as large a variety of instructional actions in response to student performance cues. Novice teachers had a lesser tendency to consider prior knowledge about subject matter content, student history and pedagogical principles during instruction. A wider variety of instructional goals were also considered by the experienced teacher. Care must be taken in generalizing these results because of the small number of participants in the study; however, the scheme for classifying student performance cues and subsequent instructional actions by teachers, is a definite contribution.

As they are teaching, teachers try to balance multiple goals, both academic and classroom management, to maintain a flow of activity and social organization. In reaching a balance, some teachers emphasize classroom management, others provide greater emphasis on academic learning. Management of learners is a major concern of teachers as they plan the instructional task. As the teaching routine is being carried out, teachers monitor student behavior. Usually, only when students are not participating or there is an unusual amount of unacceptable behavior, do teachers change their routines. It is possible that teachers, in some cases when things aren't going well, choose to deal with a problem later in future lessons. The paper by Vasa (1984) (this volume) on classroom management research, explores more completely the relationship between management of learning activities and the management of learners.

Summary of Major Findings

From the research reviewed for this paper several generalizations can be made. Teachers do not follow the "ends-means" planning models advocated by Tyler (1949) and many others. Rather they focus on content to be taught and the activities in which they will engage students. Teachers plan these elements around an instructional task. Tasks serve as mental images or scripts for teachers. These scripts are conceptualized in abbreviated fashion which helps to reduce the information processing load of teachers.

Once teachers begin lessons for groups of students, they are very reluctant to change those lessons, even when things are going poorly. Teachers use cues from students, in the form of participation and appropriate behavior, to judge how well lessons are progressing. When changes are made in lessons, they usually are minor modifications or "fine tuning." During interactive teaching, teachers' primary concerns focus on maintaining a flow of activities. There is evidence that teachers work to make the classroom activities very predictable, thus, reducing the complexity of the classroom. Maintaining order in the classroom is a major concern of teachers while making decisions both before they teach and while they are interacting with students.

Implications for Teacher Educators

1. Teacher educators need to be aware of the decision-making practices of experienced teachers. The planning models which experienced teachers use should be considered valid for the contexts in which teachers find themselves. The theoretical models can still be presented to preservice teachers

but a more balanced view of teacher planning and decision making should be presented.

2. Because of the impact of planning done early in the year on subsequent decisions and activities, teacher educators should provide more emphasis on long-range planning. Instructors of methods courses may need to change their focus from unit planning to longer range, yearly planning activities for their students. Many of these decisions, such as grouping of students, establishing course requirements, grading schemes and developing management schemes appear to be made most effectively early in the year. Knowing this before they start would help beginning teachers to a more successful start in the first year of teaching.

3. Research on teacher planning demonstrates that teachers develop a series of instructional tasks which serve as scripts for them as they interact with students. More attention should be given to assist beginning teachers in developing high quality tasks for their initial lessons as they begin to teach. Efforts need to be made to find better ways of helping teachers develop a wide repertoire of "scripts," so that during interactive teaching, teachers have a range of alternatives to consider when the activities are not successful with a group of students and so that teachers can seek to optimize their instruction.

References

Armstrong, D. G., & Savage, T. (1983). *Secondary education: An introduction.* New York: Macmillan Publishing Co., Inc.

Callahan, J., & Clark, L. H. (1977). *Teaching in the secondary school.* New York: Macmillan Publishing Co., Inc.

Clark, C., & Joyce, B. (1981). Teacher decision making and teacher effectiveness. *Flexibility in teaching.* New York: Longman, Inc.

Clark, C., & Peterson, P. L. (1976). *Teacher stimulated recall of interactive decisions.* (A research report) Palo Alto, CA: Stanford Center for Research and Development, Stanford University. (ERIC Document Reproduction Service No. ED 124 555)

Fogarty, J. L., Wang, M. C., & Creek, R. (1983, September/October). A descriptive study of experienced and novice teachers' interactive instructional thoughts and actions. *Journal of Educational Research, 77*(1).

Henson, K. (1981). *Secondary teaching methods.* Lexington, MA: D.C. Heath and Co.

Joyce, B., Brown, C. C., & Peck, L. (Eds.). (1981). *Flexibility in teaching.* New York & London: Longman, Inc.

Kim, E. C., & Kellough, R. D. (1983). *A resource guide for secondary school teaching* (3rd ed). New York: Macmillan Publishing Co., Inc.

Marx, R., & Peterson, P. L. (1981). The nature of teacher decision making. *Flexibility in teaching.* New York: Longman, Inc.

McNergney, R. F., and others. (1983, November/December). Assessing teachers' planning abilities. *Journal of Educational Research, 77(2).*

Saylor, J. G. (1982). *Who planned the curriculum? A curriculum reservoir model with historical examples.* West Lafayette, IN: Kappa Delta Pi.

Schaffarzik, J. (1976, April). *Teacher and lay participation in local curriculum change considerations.* Paper presented at annual meeting of American Educational Research Association, San Francisco, CA (ERIC Document Reproduction Service No. ED 126 620)

Shavelson, R. J. (1982, February). Review of research on teachers' pedagogical judgments, plans and decisions. Paper presented at National Invitational Conference: "Research on Teaching: Implications for Practice." Warrenton, VA (ERIC Document Reproduction Service No. ED 221 535)

Shavelson, R. J., & Stern, P. (1981, Winter). Research on teachers pedagogical thoughts, judgments, decisions, and behavior. *Review of Educational Research, 51(4),* 455-498.

Tibbetts, S. L. (1979, Spring). What ever happened to teacher autonomy? *Journal of NAWDAC, 42(3),* 8-13.

Tyler, R. W. (1949). *Basic principles of curriculum and instruction.* Chicago University Press.

Vasa, S. F. (1984). Classroom management: A selected review of the literature. (This volume)

Walter, L. J. (1979, March). How teachers plan for curriculum and instruction. *Catalyst, 2,* 3.

Zahorik, J. A. (1975, November). Teacher planning models. *Educational Leadership,* 134-139.

Classroom Management:
A Selected Review of the Literature

Stanley F. Vasa

University of Nebraska-Lincoln

Introduction

Although classroom management can be viewed from various perspectives, this paper focuses on factors relating to group management of students and cooperation between the student and the teacher. More specifically, in this paper, the definition of classroom management is limited to those managerial behaviors related to maintenance of on-task student behaviors and the reduction of off-task or disruptive behaviors (Goss & Ingersoll, 1981). As a means of organizing the discussion, classroom management is viewed from the perspectives of preparation for the year, in-class activities, and monitoring behaviors, (Figure 1); specific teacher behaviors and techniques are discussed within each of those categories. Although distinctions have been made for the purpose of the discussion, in practice these aspects of classroom management are highly interrelated.

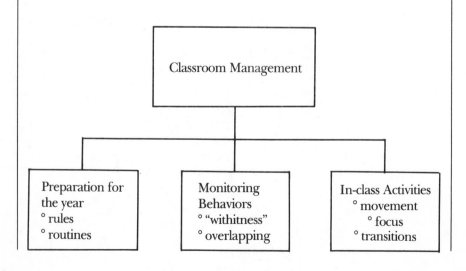

Figure 1. Categories of Classroom Management

Much of the recent work concerning classroom management has been influenced by the work of Jacob Kounin (1970), and that of Anderson, Evertson, and Emmer (1979). In his research, Kounin used videotapes to analyze teacher and student behaviors in the classroom. One study consisted of 30 self-contained classrooms, 15 first- and second-grade classrooms and 15 classrooms from grades three through five. A second videotape study consisted of 50 first- and second-grade classrooms which were selected in schools which were large enough to have at least two classrooms for a grade. Schools were selected that had, in the principal's judgment, one "good" and one "poor" classroom at the same grade level. Children were scored for work involvement and deviancy every 12 seconds but only when they were working in an academic subject. Different scorings were reported for seatwork and for recitation. Teachers' classroom management behaviors were also tabulated.

In a study with intent somewhat similar to Kounin's research, Emmer, Evertson, and Anderson (1980) compared two groups of third-grade teachers in eight elementary schools, using both beginning-of-year and follow-up observations. For comparison purposes, teachers were divided into categories of more effective and less effective managers. Rules, procedures, pupil monitoring and delivery of consequences were among the dimensions studied. Other recent research that has moved beyond Kounin has led to extensive descriptions of successful elementary and secondary classroom organization and management (Evertson, Emmer, Clements, Sanford, & Worsham 1984; Emmer, Evertson, Clements, Sanford & Worsham 1984).

Preparation for the School Year

Preparation for teaching includes a number of functions, the first of which, instructional planning, is discussed by Walter (1984) elsewhere in this monograph. Once planning is well under way, other preparatory functions assume increased importance. Among these are setting up the classroom and establishing routines.

Setting Up the Classroom

One of the major concerns of both classroom teachers and researchers about classroom management is the initiation of the school year, particularly establishing rules and guidelines for behavior during the first few weeks of school. Emmer, Evertson, and Anderson (1980); Evertson and Anderson (1979); Emmer and Evertson (1980); Evertson, Anderson, Emmer, and Clements (1980); and Emmer, Sanford, Evertson, & Clements (1981) found that more effective managers spent considerable time during the first weeks of school assisting students in learning to behave. These studies identified a number of differences between teachers judged to be effective and ineffective managers. The differences between the groups were most apparent in areas of classroom rules and procedures, monitoring of pupils, and delivery of consequences. Both groups of teachers had rules and procedures; however, the more effective teachers were distinguished from the less effective by the degree to which the rules and the procedures were integrated into a workable system.

Some of the findings which distinguished the more effective teacher were:

1. initial meetings planned for maximum contact and control,
2. well-prepared rules and procedures,
3. effective communication of rules and procedures,
4. efforts to teach rules and appropriate behavior,
5. effective monitoring of students, and
6. apparent consequences for either good or inappropriate behavior.

Routines

Yinger (1979) observed teachers making planning decisions over a period of time and analyzed the types of procedures they chose. He found that procedures whose main function is to provide continuity increased the predictability of the school day and thus played a major role in teacher effect on student time-on-task. Such routines allowed students to better predict the direction in which an activity was going and what would be expected of them (Yinger, 1980).

In Class Activities

Kounin's research, mentioned above, investigated the effects of classroom procedures and activities on students' on-task behavior (Kounin, 1970). Through study of his extensive videotapes, Kounin identified certain general categories of classroom procedures, including movement management and group focus. He then divided these general dimensions into more specific behaviors. Kounin identified two sub-categories under movement management—momentum and smoothness of movement; he identified three categories under group focus—group alerting, accountability, and format. Correlations for the sub-categories—momentum, smoothness of movement, group alerting and accountability—with (1) work involvement and (2) freedom from deviancy, under both recitation and seatwork conditions are shown in Table 1.

Table 1*

Correlations Between Teacher Behaviors and Children's Behaviors in Recitation and Seatwork Settings

| | Recitation | | Seatwork | |
	Work involvement	Freedom from deviancy	Work involvement	Freedom from deviancy
Momentum	.656**	.641	.198	.490
Smoothness	.601	.489	.382	.421
Group Alerting	.603	.442	.234	.290
Accountability	.494	.385	.002	− .035

*Adapted from Kounin (1970)

**N   49 classrooms (r of .276 significant at .05 level) Kounin (1970), p. 169.

Movement Management

Momentum. Kounin suggested that momentum could be weakened by a number of different actions: behavior overdwelling, actone overdwelling, prop overdwelling, task overdwelling, group fragmentation, and prop or actone fragmentation. Explanations of these qualities are:

Behavior overdwelling. generally categorized as "nagging" or "preaching." The teacher dwells on misbehavior beyond what is necessary.

Actone overdwelling. when a teacher concentrates or overdwells on a sub-part of an activity enough to detract from the task as a whole.

Prop overdwelling. when a teacher emphasizes a prop to the extent of losing the focus on the activity.

Task overdwelling. when the teacher elaborates explanations beyond what is required for the children to understand, to the point that children are hindered from progressing.

Group fragmentation. when a teacher has an individual student do singly what a whole group could do as a unit. By doing so, this fragmentation produces "waits" for students.

Prop or actone fragmentation. when a teacher breaks units of behavior into small components and focuses upon the sub-parts although the behavior could have been more efficiently performed as a unit.

Smoothness of Movement. In Kounin's description, smoothness of movement was weakened by stimulus-boundness, thrusts, flip-flops, dangles, and truncations. The definitions of these measures are:

Stimulus boundness. opposite of goal directedness. The teacher's ability to maintain a focus on a goal is measured in contrast to the teacher's becoming easily distracted by a stimulus to the extent that he/she forgets the goal.

Thrust. a teacher's sudden bursting in on children's activities. Timeliness is the issue.

Dangle. when a teacher starts an activity and leaves it by going to another activity. After this interruption, the teacher resumes the original activity.

Truncation. same as dangles except the teacher does not resume the original activity.

Flip-flop. measured only in transition activities. A flip-flop is when a teacher terminates one activity, starts another, and then returns to the terminated activity.

As indicated in Table 1, smoothness of movement correlated significantly with students' behaviors for both work involvement and freedom from deviancy during recitation as well as while they were engaged in seatwork. Momentum correlated with work involvement and freedom from deviancy during recitation and with freedom from deviancy during seatwork; momentum did not correlate significantly with work involvement during seatwork.

Kounin also found that momentum and smoothness correlated significantly with each other, i.e., teachers who use smooth transitions have a tendency not to slow down student progress by their behaviors.

Group Focus

In Kounin's organizational scheme, the general category of group focus was further divided into three sub-categories: group alerting, accountability and format.

Group Alerting. Techniques used for group alerting include creating suspense before calling on a child, picking reciters randomly, interspersing "mass unison" recitation along with individual recitation, calling on non-participants, and presenting new materials or methods during recitation. Negative techniques included focus on the individual to the exclusion of the group, preselection of a reciter before asking the question, and selection of reciters in a predictable order.

The results revealed that group alerting was significantly related to children's behavior in work involvement and freedom from deviancy during periods of recitation but not for either work involvement or freedom from deviancy during seatwork (see Table 1).

Accountability. Another method of achieving group focus was through accountability, which was characterized by teachers (1) asking all students to expose answers, (2) asking all students to recite in unison, (3) asking students who knew the answers to raise hands, (4) circulating and checking non-participants' work, and (5) requiring non-participants to demonstrate.

Like group alerting, the correlations of accountability with work involvement and with freedom from deviancy were significant only in recitation settings; that is, the correlations of accountability with work involvement and freedom from deviancy were not significant during seatwork. In addition, the correlation between accountability and group alerting was also significant. Both group alerting and accountability demonstrate the ability of the teacher to maintain group focus and not become immersed in working with individual students to the point of neglecting the group.

Format

Two components of instructional format were identified by Kounin: (a) the use of props and (b) the formal setup of the session (lecture, recitation, or combination). Format did not correlate significantly with either work involvement or freedom from deviancy for either recitation or seatwork.

Teacher Transitions

Another teacher behavior which the research literature shows as being important is transition from one activity to another. In a study critical to this area, Arlin (1979) addressed two research questions: Do off-task, disruptive behaviors occur when teachers make transitions from one activity to another? If so, what teacher behaviors accompany disruptive transitions and are there convenient ways to decrease the amount of disruption? Arlin defined a transition as "a teacher-initiated directive to students to end one activity and to start another."

Arlin's study focused on the amount of off-task student behavior that occurred during transition. Using naturalistic observation techniques, 50 student teachers at the elementary and junior high levels were observed in an attempt to evaluate the quality of their transitions and the resulting levels of off-task behavior. Findings showed that the rate of student off-task behavior during transitions was almost twice as great as during regular class time. However, transitions could be structured to minimize disruptive behavior. The transitions that involved the fewest pupil disruptions contained smoothness, momentum and continuity of signal. Arlin also observed that teachers often used a "steering group" in the timing of transitions and/or transitional decisions. He further suggested that the quality of transitions may serve as an easily observable indicator of the general quality of time management procedures used in the classroom.

Teacher Monitoring Behaviors

In addition to his findings related to teacher classroom behaviors, Kounin described two complex teacher characteristics that correlated substantially with work involvement and freedom from deviancy. He termed these characteristics "withitness" and "overlapping." Correlations of these characteristics with work involvement and freedom from deviancy under recitation and seatwork conditions are shown in Table 2.

Withitness

According to Kounin, "withitness" is the ability of the teacher to give the illusion to students that he/she has eyes in the back of his/her head. The "withitness" quality was measured by the following criteria:

1. ability to catch a deviancy before it spread,
2. ability to catch a deviancy before it increased in seriousness,
3. ability to desist the child causing the deviancy rather than desisting the wrong child, and
4. ability to stop the more serious deviancy rather than desisting a less serious deviancy and ignoring a more serious deviancy.

Kounin's research showed that "withitness" correlated positively with work involvement and with freedom from deviancy during both recitation and seatwork conditions (see Table 2).

Table 2

Correlations Between Teacher
Style and Children's Behavior
in Recitation and Seatwork Settings

| | Recitation | | Seatwork | |
	Work involvement	Freedom from deviancy	Work involvement	Freedom from deviancy
Withitness	.615**	.531	.307	.509
Overlapping	.460	.362	.259	.379

*Adapted from Kounin (1970).
**N 49 classrooms (r of .276 significant at .05 level) Kounin (1970), p. 169.

Overlapping

Another teacher behavior measured by Kounin was overlapping, which he defined as the teacher's ability to attend to more than one event at the same time. These overlapping events primarily occur when the teacher has to issue a desist order while at the same time working with a group of children or when the teacher is involved with one group of children and another child interrupts for some assistance.

Like withitness, overlapping correlated with work involvement and freedom from deviancy during both recitation and seatwork (see Table 2). The two aspects of teacher style, overlapping and withitness, also were intercorrelated (r = .477) (Kounin, p. 169).

Desist Techniques

In addition to the teacher behaviors and characteristics that Kounin found correlated with children's behaviors, he found one behavioral complex, desist techniques, that did not show such a relationship. Through his research Kounin attempted to determine "whether or not desist techniques made a difference in children's reactions to desist events," or "does the manner in which a teacher handles a misbehavior affect the behavioral reactions of a child to this event or not?"

In order to score these direct management techniques, Kounin coded the teachers' desists for their clarity, firmness, intensity, focus, and child treatment.

Clarity. a clearly stated desist should answer the questions who, what to stop, what to do, and why.

Firmness. the teachers' follow-through for firmness includes moving closer to the deviant student, looking at the deviant student, using a "physical assist," or using a repeat urge.

Intensity. the teacher's position and manner determined the intensity of desist.

Focus. the teacher's ability to focus positively on misbehaviors and to positively direct the deviant students into the proper activities.

Kounin concluded that, based on his data, a relationship between the qualities of teacher desist techniques and the degree of success in handling a deviancy was not supported.

The research conducted by Kounin and others provides valuable information about specific techniques which teachers can use to promote discipline and good classroom management. These management skills may allow teachers to accomplish their teaching goals; their absence may be a serious barrier to goal accomplishment. Several comments should be noted about the research. First, many of Kounin's variables are not independent and the data gathered is correlational. Second, the data may not generalize to other age-level groups of students. Finally, one wonders if well-behaved students do not produce teachers who score highly on Kounin's variables. At least a partial response to these caveats appear in a study by Borg (1977), who found that teachers given training in skills related to withitness showed a significantly greater decrease in mildly and severely disruptive behavior in their classrooms than did teachers not given such training.

Alternative
Classroom Management Models

Two recent publications have been written as an outcome of the studies conducted at the Research and Development Center for Teacher Education at the University of Texas. The two publications, *Classroom Management for Secondary Teachers* (Emmer, E., Evertson, C., Sanford, J., Clements, B., & Worsham, M., 1984), and *Classroom Management for Elementary Teachers* (Evertson, C., Emmer, E., Clements, B., Sanford, J., & Worsham, M., 1984) are attempts by the authors to put into practice classroom management procedures based on the research reviewed and conducted at the University of Texas. Contents include: organizing the classroom, choosing rules and procedures, managing student work, getting off to a good start, and organizing and conducting instruction.

A number of alternative classroom management models have been popular in the literature during the past decade (Charles, 1981). However, limited research supporting these models is available. Short descriptions of four models currently in use are provided as examples for further study. Individuals seeking information on additional models are referred to *Building Classroom Discipline from Models to Practice* by C. M. Charles (1981).

Redl's Model

Redl offers teachers insight into psychological and social forces affecting student behavior in groups and suggests to teachers specific strategies for discipline. The techniques include supporting self-control, providing situational assistance, appraising reality, and using pleasure-pain techniques designed to help teachers maintain classroom control and strengthen the emotional development in students (Redl & Wattenberg, 1959).

Assertive Discipline

Canter's model for classroom management places emphasis on the teacher as the regulator of classroom behavior and the controller of the environment by establishing and enforcing rules. The teacher serves as the dispenser of reinforcement and punishment based on predetermined rules. The model emphasizes teacher control and structure in the classroom (Canter & Canter, 1976).

Dreikurs' Model

Dreikurs (1968) places responsibilities on teachers, asking them to interpret the goals of students' misbehavior and to determine management strategies based on these goals. Formal teacher training programs implementing the model have been established by Dinkmeyer, McKay, and Dinkmeyer (1980). A major goal of the model is to assist students in becoming responsible for their behavior and actions.

Glasser's Model

Glasser (1969) provides a model for classroom management which views students as rational beings who can control their own behavior. His classroom management and discipline procedures are designed to assist the student to make good choices. His model entails developing reasonable consequences for both appropriate and inappropriate behaviors. Class rules are an essential component of this approach.

Implications
For Teacher Education

The concepts developed by Kounin and others emphasize the general behavior and classroom organization of the teacher. The approaches developed from their research provide insights for the development of teacher training programs. Transitions, early planning, rule enforcement, and effective classroom monitoring, i.e., withitness and overlapping, are concepts which are helpful to beginning teachers. A strength of these approaches is that they manage the class as a group, providing guidance for controlling misbehavior while also dealing with the remainder of the class. In addition, in each instance the approach is proactive on the part of the classroom teacher rather than reactive to the misbehavior of students. Perhaps these concepts can be a starting point for examining what further research has to offer classroom teachers in group behavior management.

The suggestion that teachers be trained to utilize such concepts as withitness and overlapping leads to several other issues. The first is whether classroom teachers can be effectively trained to utilize such strategies. Borg addressed this problem with his intervention research, but a single study does not provide definitive answers to such complex questions. However, the more recent documentation added by the researchers at the Texas R & D Center increases the credibility of this body of information.

Two additional dilemmas confronting higher education are (1) the proliferation of classroom management models, which for the most part have limited research or empirical data as support, and (2) the lack of information concerning effective matching of management models and teacher/student characteristics. These dilemmas are confounded by the question of whether teachers in training should be exposed superficially to a number of classroom management models or should receive intensive training within one or two models.

Another level of problem is the role that inherent characteristics may play in the ability of a teacher to manage classrooms. That is, the ability to use a particular classroom management style may be inherent in the style or personality of individuals. If teacher-trainees are encouraged to accept models which do not reflect their basic capabilities in the use of classroom management and discipline approaches, the chances of their success may be limited.

A minimal amount of data has been collected on the characteristics of prospective teachers and their amenability to the myriad of classroom management procedures. The formal training and practica in behavior management may need to be carefully examined to determine whether trainees have mastered the necessary skills.

References

Anderson, L., Evertson, C., & Emmer, E. (1979). *Dimensions in classroom management derived from recent research.* Austin, TX: Research and Development Center for Teacher Education. (ERIC Document Reproduction Service No. ED 175 860)

Arlin, M. (1979). Teacher transitions can disrupt time flow in classrooms. *American Educational Research Journal, 16*, 42-56.

Borg, W. (1977). Changing teacher and pupil performance with protocols. *Journal of Experimental Education, 45(3)*, 9-18.

Canter, L., & Canter, M. (1976). *Assertive discipline: A take-charge approach for today's educator.* Los Angeles: Lee Canter and Associates.

Charles, C. (1981). *Building classroom discipline: From models to practice.* New York: Longman, Inc.

Dinkmeyer, D., McKay, G., & Dinkmeyer, D. (1980). *Systematic training for effective teaching.* Circle Pines, MN: American Guidance Services.

Driekurs, R. (1968). *Psychology in the classroom.* New York: Harper & Row.

Emmer, E., & Evertson, C. (1980). *Effective management at the beginning of the school year in junior high classes.* Austin, TX: Research and Development Center for Teacher Education. (R & D Rep. No. 61079).

Emmer, E., Evertson, C., & Anderson, L. (1980). Effective classroom management at the beginning of the school year. *The Elementary School Journal, 80,* 219-231.

Emmer, E., Evertson, C., Sanford, J., Clements, B., & Worsham, M. (1984). *Classroom management for secondary teachers.* Englewood Cliffs, NJ: Prentice Hall.

Emmer, E., Sanford, J., Evertson, C., Clements, B., & Martin, J. (1981). *The classroom management improvement study: An experiment in elementary school classrooms.* Austin, TX: Research and Development Center for Teacher Education. (ERIC Document Reproduction Service No. ED 226 452)

Evertson, C., & Anderson, L. (1979). Beginning school. *Educational Horizons, 57,* 164-168.

Evertson, C., and others. (1984). *Classroom management for elementary teachers.* Englewood Cliffs, NJ: Prentice Hall.

Glasser, W. (1969). *Schools without failure.* New York: Harper & Row.

Gogg, S. S., & Ingersoll, G. H. (1981). *Management of disruptive and off-task behaviors: Selected resources.* Bloomington, IN: Indiana University. (ERIC Document Reproduction Service No. ED 200 520)

Kounin, J. (1970). *Discipline and group management in classrooms.* Malabar, FL: Robert E. Krieger Publishing Company.

Redl, F., & Wattenberg, W. (1959). *Mental hygiene in teaching.* New York: Harcourt, Brace, & World.

Walter, J. (1984). *A synthesis of research findings on teacher planning and decisionmaking.* Paper presented at the meeting of the Nebraska Teacher Education Consortium, Lincoln, NE.

Yinger, R. (1980). A study of teacher planning. *Elementary School Journal, 80*(5), 107-127.

Yinger, R. (1979). Routines in teacher planning. *Theory into Practice, 18,* 163-169.

Key Elements of Effective Teaching In the Direct Teaching Model

Roger H. Bruning

University of Nebraska-Lincoln

S ome would argue that teaching is simply unanalyzable because of its diverse aims and its complexity. Certainly, many people prefer to consider teaching as an art because a majority of the experiences, emotions, and values in teaching seem to be outside of the realm of scientific inquiry (e.g., Highet, 1957). Others, however, have begun to look more closely from a scientific perspective at the interaction that takes place in classrooms.

Initially, scientific studies provided us with information that merely piqued our interest. For example, we now know as the result of a multitude of observational studies that the typical classroom is strongly teacher-dominated and directed, with ordinarily upwards of 80 percent of the interactions coming from the teacher. Student interaction, in contrast, is quite infrequent but varies widely from student to student and from classroom to classroom. In a several hour span, some students may interact as infrequently as 4 or 5 times, while others have as many as 120 or more interactions. In a typical day, a teacher may have as many as 1000 or more contacts with students.

Other data have been equally provocative: males receive much more criticism from teachers than do females, minority group members receive more negative interactions and fewer total interactions (Civil Rights Commission, 1973), "high expectation" students receive more teacher attention (Brophy, 1983), lower SES students are criticized more (Heller & White, 1975), and attractive students are often the beneficiaries of more favorable judgments from teachers (Ross & Salvia, 1975). Elementary students, Rosenshine's data tell us, work alone about 50 to 70 percent of the time and participate in recitations only a little over 10 percent of the time (Rosenshine, 1979). Students usually spend only about 2/3 to 3/4 of the possible instructional time engaged in learning activities (Berliner, 1979), although the time spent varies greatly from classroom to classroom. And while questions have always been a part of the classroom process, their nature has changed very little in this century. About 2/3 of the questions asked by teachers are focused on factual recall of information.

We can look at data such as these with great interest and, indeed, they do provide interesting clues about classroom processes. An overriding concern of many, however, has been with finding those activities and methods that are associated with important *outcomes*. In other words, do some classroom processes lead to more desirable outcomes than others?

Intuitively, we would immediately offer an affirmative answer to this question. Attempts to pinpoint variables that are reliably associated with important classroom outcomes, however, have been noteworthy for their confusion and failure to lead to any set of instructional principles, let alone a *convincing* set of principles. Decades of instructional methods comparisons, for example, left the educational community with little more than a clear idea of the power of Hawthorne-type experimental effects and a belief that the research methods used to study process-product relationships were sadly inadequate to the task (Rosenshine, 1970; Duncan & Biddle, 1974; Good, Biddle & Brophy, 1975).

The judgment that instructional variations made little or no difference that had been or even could be documented persisted well into the 1970's in the educational research community. Large scale research projects such as that of Coleman et al., (1966) and its followups by Mosteller and Moynihan (1972) and Jencks et al., (1972) led many to the conclusion that not only might variations in instructional methods make very little difference, they may have few important effects on learning at all, at least in comparison to social influences such as that of family and socioeconomic status.

In the past 10 years, however, these judgments have been shown to be premature. A large and substantial body of information, based on converging lines of evidence, has provided support for the contention that certain instructional techniques *do* have important effects on the outcomes of learning, most particularly, on the achievement levels of students who experience the instruction. These techniques are based on a view shared by most teachers, administrators, parents, and students—that the teacher is the ultimate instructional decision-maker and leader in the classroom (Rosenshine, 1983). In this perspective, classroom management techniques and effective instruction go hand in hand through good planning, curriculum arrangement, and instruction that keeps students engaged in learning. The approaches collectively are called *direct teaching*, in reference to their emphasis on teacher control over the organization, planning, scheduling, and delivery of instruction.

Kounin's Early Research

The landmark research for this new, optimistic view of the efficacy of instruction is that of Kounin (1970). In a series of studies, Kounin focused on observations of teachers who were successful or unsuccessful as classroom managers. After an initial discovery in which Kounin found that there was little or no difference in the ability of these two groups of teachers to handle disruptive behavior when it occurred, he began to direct his attention toward the activities of the classroom that lead toward learning and away from disruption. This line of reasoning, based on use of naturalistic inquiry methods to determine differences between groups of individuals, was a method used by several large scale research projects that have led to a much clearer conception of what constitutes effective instruction.

Kounin's research pointed to several important ways that effective classroom managers differed from ineffective classroom managers. The difference came not in their ability to handle disruptions once they occurred, but in problem *prevention* based on good management techniques. Successful managers were successful because they kept their students engaged in productive classroom work most of the time. Their techniques included the following:

1. *Preparation and organization.* Successful managers were much better prepared and organized. Their activity showed clear effects of pre-planning.

2. *Smooth transitions between activities.* In contrast to ineffective managers, the skilled classroom managers made smooth, rapid shifts from one classroom activity to the next. The poor managers, on the other hand, were involved in long delays, awkward pauses, and frequent returns to previously given instructions. The ineffective managers showed little in the way of a predictable classroom routine; the effective teachers' classrooms had well-defined routines that were followed each class period.

3. *Overlapping.* The skilled managers showed the capacity to do more than one activity at once without disrupting either. For instance, a group activity would continue while the teacher monitored individuals working on seatwork.

4. *Active student involvement and accountability.* Skilled managers asked more questions and used a less predictable pattern of questions to hold student interest. Students in these classrooms were clearly held accountable for their performance, in contrast to students in poor managers' classes.

5. *Appropriate seatwork.* The good managers selected seatwork that was at an appropriate level of difficulty, neither too hard nor too easy, and chose materials for seatwork that were clearly relevant to the concept covered in the classroom. Ineffective teachers were much less skillful in choosing appropriate seatwork.

6. *"Withitness."* This whimsical name describes a quality that relates to early, correct, and appropriate reactions to potential disruptions. Effective managers were much more skillful in this area than ineffective ones. They did not over-react emotionally, they identified the right

students as problem sources, and they reacted quickly in keeping small disturbances from becoming large discipline problems.

7. *Group alerting.* By a variety of techniques, good managers kept students "on their toes" and alert. The techniques they used ranged from making challenges, to looking around the class and using rigid questioning orders.

The Texas Teacher Effectiveness Project

B y mid-decade, another large-scale project had been completed and reported: the Texas Teacher Effectiveness Project (Brophy, 1973; Brophy & Evertson, 1976). This study focused on second and third-grade teachers who had been teaching at their respective grade levels for four or more years. These grade levels were chosen for a variety of reasons, but primarily because at this level it was possible to identify appropriate criteria of teacher effectiveness and to find teachers who showed consistency on these criteria. Another consideration was the teachers' probable effect on young children.

The study focused on the differential ability of teachers to produce achievement in their students. Standardized test scores were selected as the least biased of possible measures of achievement. A singularly important innovation in this study was the identification of teachers who exhibited *consistent* patterns of high or low pupil achievement. Previous studies, as Rosenshine pointed out in his 1970 review (Rosenshine, 1970), almost all had failed to take into account the stability of achievement over time; the inherent instability of short term effects made finding reliable process differences difficult if not impossible. Thus, in the Brophy and Evertson study, achievement gain scores were computed for three years' results in language arts and mathematics sections of the Metropolitan Achievement Tests, statistically adjusted for student ability. Data were selected for the 40 teachers who showed the greatest general consistency; of these, 31 were finally selected for intensive study in the first year and 28 for the second.

Stage two of the Texas project involved classroom observation in the classes of these "consistent" teachers and use of ratings, checklists, interviews, and questionnaires. Observations covered from 10 to 30 hours per teacher per year. The result was a massive body of data; a total of 580 variables were available for analysis. The question of interest, then, was the following: what variables, if any, are reliably associated with consistently high or low achievement?

Brophy and Evertson's results largely confirmed the earlier observations of Kounin. Student engagement in lessons was the key to successful classroom achievement. The successful teachers ran smooth, wellpaced lessons with a minimum of interruptions. Transitions were rapid and activities overlapped with one another in successful teachers' classes. Students of these successful teachers were also provided with more appropriate seatwork on which they worked more steadily. As Kounin had found earlier, Brophy and Evertson noted that classroom teachers who were successful were more aware of events in the classroom; they were more active and visually checked the classroom more frequently. Successful teachers made fewer errors in blaming the wrong child or in waiting too long to intervene in problem behavior situations. The successful teachers had relatively few rules, but what rules they had were clear and well explained. There were relatively few *ad hoc* decisions to disrupt classroom activity.

The successful teachers also differed on certain personality and attitude dimensions. In contrast to unsuccessful managers, successful teachers believed they were in charge of their own classrooms and that their goals for their classrooms were important. They made it their business to see that students learned; there was a clearly present belief in the ability of their students to learn. The successful teachers viewed their students quite realistically. While they enjoyed being with students, they did not take an overly romantic view of them nor were they negative toward them. Their view, in other words, was likely to be professionally matter-of-fact.

An interesting set of findings related to socioeconomic (SES) differences in students. Successful teachers in high SES classrooms tended to adopt patterns that reduced high levels of competitiveness and sometimes even suppressed certain students' overenthusiastic responding. Occasional negative feedback was given by successful teachers to high SES students. In contrast, successful teachers in the lower SES classrooms adopted a much more highly structured, supportive posture. Teachers who were successful here worked very patiently, waited always for responses, and liberally praised student effort, even if the answers were not completely correct.

Follow-Through
Classroom Observation Evaluations

At about the same time, Jane Stallings (Stallings, 1974; 1975) was reporting on the results of a massive study of Project Follow-Through, conducted to evaluate the effects of planned variations among the several instructional models implemented in the Follow-Through project. In this evaluation, four first-grade and four third-grade classrooms were observed in each of 36 towns and cities. A component of this large investigation is of particular interest in the present discussion; namely, how do classroom processes relate to classroom outcome measures, including achievement. In mathematics, several variables related to (1) the opportunity to engage in math-related activity and (2) the amount of time spent learning were positively correlated with mathematics achievement. In reading, the amount of time spent in school and the amount of time spent reading were correlated with reading achievement.

In summary, children who performed well on tests of reading and mathematics were those who were in classrooms where *the most time was spent on developing academic skills.* Several variables combined to create these effects:

duration of the school day, average time each child spent in reading or mathematics or related subjects, and the frequency of academic verbal interactions. (See papers by Egbert & Kluender and Stallings, this volume.) This component of Stallings' research is highly consistent with the findings of the Texas project and the earlier work of Kounin; as time on task increases, as it will in well-organized and smoothly-run classrooms, achievement is likely to increase.

Beginning
Teacher Evaluation Study

B erliner (1979) examined the effect that time-on-task has on academic achievement. Since students spend so much of their time in seatwork (Rosenshine, 1979), seatwork is of considerable importance in how much students achieve. Quality, focus, and time spent on seatwork are likely to make a major difference in the amount of achievement that a teacher can expect from his or her students.

In Berliner's research, the aim was to derive an estimate of "academic learning time" per day and per school year. Interestingly, a 150 day school year estimate was used as the basis for judging the total available school days per year, because of the judgment that the standard 180 day school year is significantly shortened by testing, holiday activities, and many other intrusions that commonly compete with instructional time.

Berliner and his associates observed from 74 to 97 days in the various classes. In second grade mathematics classes, the percentages of time engaged in work on mathematics curriculum materials and activities ranged from 61% to 78%. In fifth-grade reading, time spent in reading curriculum and activities ranged from 75% to 84% of available time. When time was estimated for student interaction with low error-rate materials, which promote the highest achievement, a variable called "academic learning time" is the result. Academic learning time is positively related to achievement (Fisher, Filby, Marliave, Cohen, Dishaw, Moore, and Berliner, 1979). In total, the "daily" estimates of academic learning time ranged from 12 to 23 minutes per day in mathematics for the second graders and 24 to 59 minutes per day for the fifth grade classes in reading. Per year the time estimates for academic learning time range from 33 to 58 hours in mathematics, and from 60 to 148 hours in reading. According to this and earlier studies, academic learning time is closely associated with achievement. (See paper by Egbert and Kluender, this volume.)

How does one improve achievement through more academic learning time? According to Gage and Berliner (1979), the most simple and direct method is to allocate more time to academic activities. Teachers vary widely in their ability to use time efficiently, and increased time can usually be found in the school day for academic activities. Several methods are related to more efficient use of time (Gage & Berliner, 1979; p. 629). Among these are clear-cut rules that permit students to make decisions without having to consult their teachers, the teacher's moving around the room to oversee seatwork, minimizing verbal directions, and perhaps most importantly, selecting seat work that has intrinsic value, is interesting, and is yet at an easy enough level that it insures a high degree of success.

The Missouri
Mathematics Effectiveness Study

Good and Grouws, in a 1979 *Journal of Educational Psychology* article (Good and Grouws, 1979) reported on the results of a study in which teachers had been *trained* to implement a program of direct teaching. In this large-scale project involving 40 fourth-grade classsrooms, a large number of features uncovered in earlier correlational work on effective and ineffective teachers were incorporated into a systematic training program. The question about correlates of teaching effectiveness was now posed experimentally: Do teachers who have been trained in specific behaviors produce higher academic achievement in their students? The answer, based on the results of this study and now confirmed in several other experimental studies (e.g., Anderson, Evertson & Brophy, 1979; Evertson, Emmer, Sanford & Clements, 1982; Emmer, Evertson, Sanford & Clements, 1982) is almost certainly "yes." The results appear to be quite general for elementary grades up through junior high school.

In the study by Good and Grouws (1979), 40 teachers were divided into two groups. One group participated in two 90-minute training sessions organized around a 45-page manual which described a systematic method for teaching mathematics. Control teachers were instructed to continue in their own instructional methods through the period of the study, which lasted about two and one-half months. In this period, all teachers, experimental and control, were observed six times.

Key instructional behaviors in the model, as outlined by Good and Grouws (1979) and summarized in Good and Brophy (1980) are presented in Table 1. These key behaviors guided the activities of the teachers during the duration of the project.

Table 1

Summary of Key Instructional Behaviors in the Missouri Direct Teaching Model

1. **REVIEW**
   Review concepts associated with the homework
   Collect and deal with homework assignments
2. **DEVELOPMENT**
   Promote student understanding
   Active interaction
   Assess student comprehension
3. **SEATWORK**
   Provide uninterrupted, successful practice
   Check the students' work
4. **HOMEWORK ASSIGNMENT**
   Assign every period except Fridays
   About 15 minutes of work to be done at home
   Include one or two review problems
5. **SPECIAL REVIEWS**
   Weekly review for 1/2 period on Mondays
   Focus on skills learned during the previous week
   Monthly review conducted every 4th Monday
   Focus on concepts learned since last monthly review

Results of the Missouri Teacher Effectiveness Project showed a strong relationship of the implementation of behaviors from the model and achievement, as measured by gain scores on the mathematics subtest of a standardized achievement test. Several of the variables that showed relationships to student achievement are shown in Table 2. Most relate directly, as can be seen, to features of the direct teaching model. Conducting review, assigning homework, assigning seatwork, and guiding seatwork all show positive influences on achievement. Equally interesting were data on control teachers' use of these techniques: homework was assigned very infrequently (13%), not often checked (20%), mental computations were not often practiced (6%), and seatwork was not often actively directed at the beginning (43%). The higher degree of implementation by the experimental group teachers after training, however, resulted in substantial changes in student achievement.

Table 2
Selected Actions of Teachers and Mathematics Achievement of Their Students

ACTION	r with ACHIEVEMENT	NOW DOING*
Conduct Review	.37	62%
Develop Concepts During Review	.57	37%
Make Homework Assignments	.49	13%
Check Homework	.54	20%
Work on Mental Computation	.48	6%
Assign Seatwork	.27	56%
Actively Start Student Seatwork	.32	43%

*Percent of teachers in control group performing specified action

SOURCE: Adapted from Good and Grouws, The Missouri Mathematics Effectiveness Project (1979).

As mentioned previously, the features of the Missouri direct teaching model have now been confirmed in a number of experimental studies (see Rosenshine, 1979). This is not to say, however, that all aspects of the model are equally important, that all parts of the model must be implemented in order to achieve success, or that the model covers all important aspects of the classroom organization and management process.

Brophy's Research
On Expectations and Use of Praise

Brophy has outlined a number of factors that characterize effective teachers' expectations of themselves and students (Brophy & Putnam, 1979). In general, effective teachers have:

1. Realistic expectations of themselves and students.
2. Enjoyment of students, but within a teacher-student relationship.
3. Clarity concerning roles and behavior and about what will and will not be tolerated.
4. Positive, high expectations of achievement.
5. Positive, high expectations of pro-social behavior, with use of prescriptive information rather than personal criticism as the main method of influence.
6. Consistency of rule enforcement.
7. Patience and determination, in that a goal, once determined for students, is not abandoned.

Expectations of students, however, differ tremendously among teachers in general, Brophy found; his research also has shown that teacher behavior often varies widely depending on the expectations that they hold for given students. Key findings from this research are presented in Table 3. The results show quite clearly the "natural" tendencies of teachers to select actions based on their beliefs about the ability of their students. Thus, any training program that would maximize its effects would need to take into account such tendencies on the part of teachers to govern their behavior according to their expectations. Questioning, for example, is a key activity in direct teaching, and to the extent that teachers are less effective in questioning with low expectation students, their training would have been incomplete. Similarly, the tendency to praise lows less often and to criticize them more than high expectation students goes directly counter to other findings (e.g., Brophy, 1979) that have shown that low SES students (likely to be over-represented among low expectation students) benefit most from high levels of praise and encouragement, but are less likely to achieve under conditions in which strong support is not present.

Table 3
Teacher Expectations and Teacher Behavior
Toward Low and High Expectations Students

FOR LOW EXPECTATION STUDENTS (LOWS), TEACHERS WILL OFTEN:
1. Wait less time for lows to answer questions
2. Give lows the answer or call on someone else
3. Provide inappropriate reinforcement
4. Criticize lows more than highs for failure
5. Praise lows less than highs for success
6. Fail to give lows feedback on their public responses
7. Interact with lows less and pay less attention to them overall
8. Call on lows less often in class
9. Ask for lower performance levels from lows
10. Smile less, have less eye contact, and have fewer attentive postures toward lows

SOURCE: Adapted from Brophy, J., Research on the self-fulfilling prophecy and teacher expectations (1983a).

Among the many associated findings from the series of studies on teaching have been several on the effective use of praise in the classroom. Many studies of reinforcement made little or no distinction among types of praise that would or would not be effective, as focus was placed on uses of such methods as token systems, group contingencies, and verbal reinforcement as universally applicable in changing behavior. Brophy (1981), in summarizing work from several studies of classroom interventions and achievement, adopts a functional analytical approach to selecting what and what will not constitute effective praise in the classroom. In other words, what kinds of praise have been shown to produce increased achievement and what uses of praise have been shown to be consistently associated with lower levels of achievement? A summary of Brophy's findings is shown in Table 4. As has been emphasized in the behavioral literature, effective praise must be contingent. Praise, in order to be effective, must focus on significant achievement and performance and have a *task orientation*. A major new finding is that effective praise is seldom public praise. Most effective for increasing achievement is *private* praise, especially that given in teacher-initiated contacts.

Table 4
Guidelines for Effective Uses of Praise in the Classroom

EFFECTIVE PRAISE . . .	INEFFECTIVE PRAISE . . .
1. is contingent	1. is random and unpredictable
2. is spontaneous and genuine	2. is bland, delivered by "formula"
3. specifies the accomplishment	3. is global and untargeted
4. is given for significant achievement	4. is given without regard for effort
5. focuses attention on student performance	5. focuses attention on teacher as authority figure
6. has a within-task orientation	6. has an external orientation
7. is privately given	7. is public and comparative

SOURCE: Adapted from Brophy, J., Teacher Praise: A Functional Analysis (1981).

Summary of Effective Teaching in a
Direct Teaching Approach

The mass of correlational studies that laid the groundwork for a much better understanding of the teaching variables that affect student achievement and the experimental studies that have confirmed organizational and interactional variables as critical to achievement have added greatly to our potential ability to develop effective teachers. Although there is much to learn about teaching, it is not unreasonable to say that giant strides have been made in the past decade in understanding the classroom process and the relationship of variables in that process to achievement.

Key elements of the effective teacher's approach within a direct teaching model are summarized in Table 5. They paint a picture of a teacher who is guided by a firm view of what teaching is and what one's goals for teaching might be. They show a teacher who understands his or her students and who possesses a high level of organizational skill and sensitivity to classroom happenings. They indicate a teacher who can select activities for learning that are at an appropriate level for students (see paper by Walter, this volume) and who pays attention to giving students positive feedback on their accomplishments, not for their submissiveness. They also portray a teacher who is sensitive to the social structure of the classroom, using praise in a responsible, private, and nondivisive way to encourage attention to academic accomplishments and to reward true academic achievement.

Table 5
Characteristics of Effective Teachers in a
Direct Teaching Model

EFFECTIVE TEACHERS WILL:
1. Have a sense of personal responsibility for their classrooms
2. Have realistic attitudes toward their students
3. Run classrooms that are smooth and almost automatic
4. Have a quality called "withitness"
5. Make appropriate seatwork assignments
6. Make and check homework assignments
7. Communicate clearly defined classroom rules
8. Pace their instruction according to student background and ability
9. Give praise for students during teacher-initiated contacts

SOURCE: Adapted from Kounin, Rosenshine, Good and Brophy (1970-1983).

The experimental studies that have explored elements of a direct teaching model should be most encouraging to those in teacher education, because they clearly hold forth the potential for training preservice teachers in a set of skills that have been shown to relate to students' academic achievement. (See papers by Egbert and by Billups, this volume.) They are soundly based in research. These skills are not mysterious nor are they impossible to learn. In fact, they match well with common sense and one can only wonder at their extraordinary neglect in much of teaching at all levels: elementary, secondary, and postsecondary. At last, however, we seem to have a well-founded body of information at our disposal as teachers of preservice teachers. We now not only have the opportunity to impart it to our students, but to apply this knowledge with good effect in our own teacher-student interactions in our own classrooms.

References

Anderson, L., Evertson, C., & Brophy, J. E. (1979). An experimental study of effective teaching in first grade reading groups. *Elementary School Journal, 79*, 199-223.
Berliner, D. (1979). Tempus educare. In P. L. Peterson & H. J. Wahlberg (Eds.), *Research on teaching: Concepts, findings, and implications*. Berkeley, CA: McCutchan.
Billups, L. (1984). Research and the classroom teacher. (This volume.)
Brophy, J. (1973). The stability of teacher effectiveness. *American Educational Research Journal, 10*, 245-252.
Brophy, J. (1979). Teacher behavior and its effects. *Journal of Educational Psychology, 71*, 733-750.

Brophy, J. (1981). Teacher praise: A functional analysis. *Review of Educational Research, 51*, 5-32.

Brophy, J. (1983a). Research on the self-fulfilling prophecy and teacher expectations. *Journal of Educational Psychology, 75*, 631-661.

Brophy, J. (1983b). Classroom organization and management. *Elementary School Journal, 83*, 265-285.

Brophy, J., & Evertson, C. M. (1976). *Learning from teaching: A developmental perspective.* Boston: Allyn & Bacon.

Brophy, J., & Putnam, J. (1979). Classroom management in the elementary grades. In D. Duke (Ed.), *Classroom management.* The 78th Yearbook of the National Society for the Study of Education, Part II. Chicago: University of Chicago Press.

Brophy, J., Rohrkemper, M., Rashid, H., & Goldberger, M. (1983). Relationships between teachers' presentations of classroom tasks and students' engagement in those tasks. *Journal of Educational Psychology, 75*, 544-552.

Civil Rights Commission. (1973). *Teachers and Students Report V. Differences in Teacher Interaction with Mexican-American and Anglo Students.* Washington, DC: U.S. Government Printing Office.

Coleman, J. S., Campbell, E. Q., Hobson, C. J., McPartland, J., Mood, A. M., Weinfeld, F. D., & York, R. L. (1966). *Equality of educational opportunity.* Washington, DC: U.S. Government Printing Office.

Dunkin, M. J., & Biddle, B. J. (1974). *The study of teaching.* New York: Holt, Rinehart, & Winston.

Egbert, R. L. (1984). The role of research in teacher education. (This volume.)

Egbert, R. L., & Kluender, M. M. (1984). Time as an element in school success. (This volume.)

Emmer, E., Evertson, C. M., & Anderson, I. (1980). Effective management at the beginning of the school year. *Elementary School Journal, 80*, 219-231.

Emmer, E. T., Evertson, C. M., Sanford, J., & Clements, B. S. (1982). *Improving classroom management: An experimental study in junior high classrooms.* Austin: R & D Center for Teacher Education, University of Texas.

Evertson, C. M., & Emmer, E. (1982). Effective management at the beginning of the school year in junior high classes. *Journal of Educational Psychology, 74*, 485-498.

Evertson, C. M., Anderson, L., & Brophy, J. (1978). *Final report of process-outcome relationships* (Vol. 1) (Report No. 4061). Austin, TX: R & D Center for Teacher Education, University of Texas.

Evertson, C. M., Emmer, E. T., Sanford, J., & Clements, B. S. (1982). *Improving classroom management: An experimental study in elementary classrooms.* Austin, R & D Center for Teacher Education, University of Texas.

Fisher, C. W., Filby, N. A., Marliave, R., Cohen, L. S., Dishaw, M. M., Moore, J. E., & Berliner, D. C. (1978). *Teaching behaviors, academic learning time, and student achievement: Final report of Phase III-B, beginning teacher eval-*

uation study (Tech. Report V-1). San Francisco: Far West Laboratory for Education Research & Development.

Gage, N. L., & Berliner, D. C. (1979). *Educational psychology* (2nd ed.). Boston: Houghton Mifflin.

Good, T. L., & Brophy, J. E. (1980). *Educational psychology: A realistic approach* (2nd ed.). New York: Holt, Rinehart, & Winston.

Good, T. L., & Grouws, D. A. (1979). The Missouri Mathematics Effectiveness Project: An experimental study in fourth-grade classroom. *Journal of Educational Psychology, 71*, 355-362.

Good, T. L., Biddle, B. J., & Brophy, J. E. (1975). Teachers make a difference. New York: Holt, Rinehart, & Winston.

Heller, M. S., & White, M. A. (1975). Rates of teacher verbal approval and disapproval to higher and lower ability classes. *Journal of Educational Psychology, 67*, 796-800.

Highet, G. (1957). *The art of teaching.* New York: Vintage.

Jencks, C., Smith, M., Ackland, H., Bane, M. J., Cahen, D., Gintis, H., Heyns, B., & Michelson, S. (1972). *Inequality. A reassessment of family and schooling in America.* New York: Basic Books.

Kounin, J. (1970). *Discipline and group management in classrooms.* New York: Holt, Rinehart, & Winston.

Mosteller, F., & Moynihan, D. (Eds.). (1972). *On equality of educational opportunity.* New York: Vintage.

Peterson, P., Marx, C. W., & Clark, R. M. (1978). Teacher planning, teacher behavior, and student achievement. *American Educational Research Journal, 15*, 417-143.

Rosenshine, B. (1970). The stability of teacher effects on student achievement. *Review of Educational Research, 40*, 647-662.

Rosenshine, B. (1979). The third cycle of research on teacher effects: Content covered, academic engaged time, and direct instruction. In P. L. Peterson & H. J. Wahlberg (Eds.), *Research on teaching: Concepts, findings, and implications.* Berkeley, CA: McCutchan.

Rosenshine, B. (1983). Teaching functions in instructional programs. *Elementary School Journal, 83*, 335-351.

Ross, M., & Salvia, J. (1975). Attractiveness as a biasing factor in teacher judgments. *American Journal of Mental Deficiency, 80*, 96-98.

Stallings, J. A., & Kaskowitz, D. (1974). *Follow-through classroom observation evaluation 1972-1973.* Menlo Park, CA: Stanford Research Institute.

Stallings, J. A. (1975). Implications and child effects of teaching practices in follow-through classrooms. *Monograph of the Society for Research in Child Development, 40*(Serial No. 163).

Stallings, J. A. (1984). Imlications from the research on teaching for teacher preparation. (This volume.)

Walter, L. J. (1984). A synthesis of research findings on teacher planning and decision-making. (This volume.)

Time as an Element in School Success

Robert L. Egbert and Mary M. Kluender

University of Nebraska-Lincoln

Psychologists interested in the learning process always have considered time, or number of repetitions, to be a potentially important variable in the amount of learning that occurs. In some studies psychologists have made time (repetitions) an independent variable, while in others they have controlled for time or repetitions, but they have never ignored the issue. (See, for example, Thorndike, 1931; McGeoch, 1942.) Educational psychologists who have extended laboratory studies of rats, pigeons and people to classroom and school research have likewise considered time an important variable and have either made it an independent variable, or have controlled for it. (See, for example, Forlano, 1936; Frandsen, 1957).

Educational curriculum planners also usually have appeared to think of time as an important variable in learning, as when they have assigned more elementary school time to tool subjects, e.g., reading and arithmetic, than they have to such subjects as music and physical education, without regard for the time required to acquire mastery. That is, by assigning relatively more time to reading and arithmetic than to music and physical education, curriculum planners have demonstrated that they value elementary school children achieving mastery of reading and arithmetic more than they do similar mastery of music and physical education. However, curriculum planners at other times have appeared unaware of the importance of time in the learning process and of the research evidence demonstrating that time is an important variable in learning. An example is when they have subtracted from the elementary school time devoted to tool subjects, rather than lengthening the school day, in order to provide a broadened curriculum.

Within the last few years, almost unrelated events and concerns have taken place in educational research and in educational planning that have caused school time to become a high priority issue. In educational research, three important documents were published: (1) John Carroll's theoretical paper (1963) stating that the degree of learning that occurs is a function of the amount of time spent learning divided by the amount of time required for learning, (2) Coleman's suggestion (1966) that the nature of schooling does not make a difference in educational outcomes, and (3) Wiley and Harnischfeger's analysis (1974) of a sixth-grade sample of Coleman's Detroit Metropolitan Area data in which they found that amount of schooling (attendance x length of school day x days in school year) bore a substantial relationship to school achievement. The Wiley and Harnischfeger analysis and model, which at least partially refuted Coleman's conclusions, began a revolution in the way educational researchers thought about the instructional process. More recent research has established further support for the Carroll and Wiley-Harnischfeger models, e.g., Karweit and Slavin (1981), Daniels and Haller (1981).

In educational planning there was not an easily identified set of publications or events that began the trend of concern about how school time is spent; instead, there developed a gradually spreading concern that one reason for lowered achievement scores was a diffusion of the curriculum in which less time was spent on such essential subjects as English, mathematics and science in order to allow time for elective subjects (Harnischfeger, 1980; *A Nation at Risk*, 1983).

The single most important research base for the present interest in the assignment and use of school time is the California Beginning Teacher Evaluation Study (BTES). Initiated in 1970 to identify generic teacher competencies and evaluate teacher education programs through follow-up of their graduates, this project continued for almost ten years and conducted broad ranging research concerning teacher and student behaviors and student achievement, largely in the classrooms of experienced teachers. Academic Learning Time, the amount of time the student spends in an academic task that s/he can perform with high success, became a central concept in the research (Powell, 1980; Fisher et al., 1980).

The Time to Learn Concept

Over the past ten years, several measures of school time have been designed. Each one is important for different dimensions of research and practice, but not all of those that are important for research or for school district management are critical for understanding what takes place in a specific classroom. Thus, information produced in the Wiley-Harnischfeger model (1974) mentioned earlier, which refers to quantity of time available for the teacher, is useful to researchers studying the achievement value added by increasing the quantity of time available for learning and to school boards and school administrators who are interested in raising achievement levels in their schools, but it lacks the detail necessary for either building or classroom analysis. However, several other studies have used definitions useful at the classroom level.

The BTES is an example of a study using time definitions useful in classrooms. The BTES used three measures of time—allocated time (the amount of time allotted to the teaching of a given subject), engaged time (the amount of time that a child/student is on task), and academic learning time (Rosenshine, 1980). Each of these measures describes time at a more restricted level of generality than the three components of the Wiley-Harnischfeger model. A comprehensive model that includes elements from both levels of generality might have at least five components:

1. *Assigned time*—the amount of time that the school district determines is available for the school. (Length of school day x days in school year.)
2. *Average daily attendance*—as a percent of the potential.
3. *Allocated time*—the amount of time that the teacher or the school allots to a given content area. This might be a year-long allocation for a subject area or it could be the amount available for a unit or topic within the subject area.
4. *Engaged time.*
5. *Academic learning time.*

Each of these measures or components varies across districts, schools and classes. In fact, one of the more immediately usable results from the time-to-learn research is knowledge of the wide variation from school to school and class to class on the different measures of time. This has permitted researchers and practitioners to view classrooms in the context of both average time and ranges of time.

Dimensions of the time variation have been described by a number of authors. Examples are:

1. As reported by Harnischfeger and Wiley (1976), Mann (1928) summarized daily mean subject area time allocations in minutes. For the third grade, these were: reading—70.4; language—62.8; social studies and science—31.8; arithmetic—39.2; arts—33.4; physical education and recess-38.0; general—7.4; and nonacademic—24.4.
2. Wiley and Harnischfeger (1974) reported a range in the amount of time available for sixth-grade classroom teachers as ranging from 710 to 1150 hours.
3. Rosenshine (1980) summarized BTES data (Table 1, below) as showing that, at the second-grade level, the allocated, in-class time was divided into (a) two hours and fifteen minutes (fifty-seven percent) for academic activities, (b) fifty-five minutes (twenty-four percent) for nonacademic instructional activities, and (c) forty-four minutes (nineteen percent) for noninstructional activities. At the fifth-grade level, these times were two hours and fifty minutes (sixty percent), one hour and five minutes (twenty-three percent) and forty-five minutes (seventeen percent) respectively.

Table 1
Average Allocated Time per Day in Different Activities

Time Category	Grade 2		Grade 5	
	Minutes	Percentage	Minutes	Percentage
Academic Activities	2'12"	57%	2'51"	60%
Nonacademic Activities	55"	24%	1'05"	23%
Noninstructional Activities	44"	19%	47"	17%
Major In-class Time	3'51"	100%	4'44"	100%

*Adapted from Rosenshine (1980)

In addition to the in-class time, Rosenshine also reported approximately one-and-a-quarter hours for lunch and breaks, bringing the average second-grade day to just over five hours in length; the sixth-grade day to approximately six hours.

4. Within the overall allocated time in the BTES, there was considerable variation among teachers. This is shown in Table 2 (Table 5.3 in Rosenshine, 1980). Not only was the allocated time substantially higher for the three high teachers than it was for the three low teachers, the engaged rate was higher for those teachers who allocated the greatest amount of time to academic instruction. Furthermore, the pattern was consistent for both reading and mathematics.

Table 2
Differences in Academic Engaged Minutes in Highest, Average and Lowest Classrooms

	Reading			Mathematics			Total	
	Allo-cated	Engage-ment rate	Engaged minutes	Allo-cated	Engage-ment rate	Engaged minutes	Allocated time	Engaged minutes
Second grade								
High3	1'45"	81%	1'25"	35"	82%	30"	2'20"	1'55"
Average	1'30"	73%	1'04"	36"	71%	26"	2'06"	1'30"
Low 3	1'00"	72%	43"	30"	75%	22"	1'30"	1'05"
Fifth grade								
High 3	2'10"	80%	1'45"	53"	86%	45"	3'03"	2'30"
Average	1'50"	74%	1'20"	44"	74%	35"	2'25"	1'55"
Low 3	1'25"	63%	1'05"	38"	63%	22"	2'03"	1'25"

*Adapted from Rosenshine (1980).

5. Karweit and Slavin (1981) found a range of scheduled time in mathematics in 18 second to fifth-grade classes in the same district of from 240 to 300 minutes with a mean of 269 minutes. Of the scheduled time, 176 to 308 minutes (a mean of 239 minutes) were *actually* allocated to teaching. Of that time, 142 to 290 (a mean of 217) minutes were used in mathematics instruction. (Table 3)

The engaged time ranged from 134 to 244 minutes with a mean of 183. Thus, the time lost each week between allocated and engaged time was a mean of 86 minutes, with a range of from 56 to 140 minutes.

Table 3*
Scheduled, Actual, and Instructional Time for Elementary School Mathematics

	Scheduled Minutes	Actual Minutes	Instructional Minutes	Engaged Minutes	Lost Minutes
Mean	269	239	217	183	86
Range	240-300	176-308	142-290	134-244	56-140

*Adapted from Karweit and Slavin (1981).

Several authors have reported classroom time by process categories. At perhaps the simplest level, Rosenshine (1980) divided time into teacher-led and seatwork categories. Within these two categories, Rosenshine noted that engaged percentage rate was higher for teacher-led portions of the program (the low eighties) than for seatwork (approximately 70 percent). DeVault (1977) analyzed classroom time in three subject areas: (1) language, (2) arts, and (3) mathematics and in four categories (1) supervised whole class, (2) supervised subgroup, (3) supervised individual, and (4) unsupervised individual. Stallings (1980) used an even more complex set of process categories with which to analyze reading instruction.

One of the more important concepts within the time-to-learn structure is the way in which time gets subtracted from the maximum time available by the various actors—administrators, teachers, and pupils (students). Although relatively less research effort has been devoted to studying this dimension, there are some useful studies. Again, at the simplest level, Rosenshine (1980), reporting data from the BTES, gave two different sorts of nonengaged time: (1) interim and wait, and (2) off-task. From the BTES data, Rosenshine concluded that a certain amount of "interim and wait" time is a fact of life in all classrooms, even the most efficient. This conclusion was based on the observation that time lost for this reason was very similar across "high," "average" and "low" classrooms. On the other hand, Rosenshine noted that the amount of off-task time varies considerably from one classroom to another. Thus, it would appear that changing the instruction and management processes may result in more engaged time, not necessarily through reduction of interim and wait time, but through reduction of off-task time.

Karweit and Slavin (1981) separated the time lost into that which is lost by (1) intrusion, (2) procedure, and (3) inattention. "Intrusion" is time lost to external forces. For example, in one school, math instruction occurred just before lunch, and several minutes were lost from mathematics instruction each day to permit the children to be lined up for lunch. "Procedure" is time lost by such classroom procedures as handing in assignments, picking up books, and taking roll. "Inattention," of course, is the pupil focusing on something other than the lesson. Karweit and Slavin reported an average of 30.5 minutes lost per week due to intrusion, 20.6 due to procedure, and 34.0 due to inattention for a total average loss of 85 minutes from the 269 minutes available for instruction. Of course, as mentioned above, the range of time lost varied substantially from one classroom to another. Furthermore, the time lost for each of the three causes also varied considerably—from zero to sixty-four minutes per week for intrusion, from four to thirty-two minutes for procedures, and from eighteen to fifty-seven minutes for inattention. It is of at least passing interest to note that the classroom that had the highest loss from intrusion also had the highest loss from procedures and the third (of twelve) highest loss from inattention.

The Mid-continent Regional Educational Laboratory (McREL) (1983) has developed a comprehensive scheme for representing the total time available for the school and then subtracting the amounts of time that disappear, leaving as a remainder the time available for student learning. Table 4 contains a comparative summary of the concepts involved in the Rosenshine, Karweit and Slavin, and McREL reports.

Table 4
Summary of Concepts on How Time is Lost
Terms Used in Different Sources

	Concept		
	Administrator Subtraction	Teacher Subtraction	Student Subtraction
Rosenshine		Interim & Wait	Off-task
Karweit & Slavin	Intrusion	Procedure	Inattention
McREL	Non-Academic Building Activities	Non-Academic Class Activities	Student Iattentiveness

Uses of the Time to Learn Concept

Time to Learn and Achievement

One of the key questions that researchers have asked about time is, "What is the relationship between how class time is spent and student achievement gains?" This broad question has at least two sub-issues. The first issue is the relationship between the allocation of time and student achievement; the second issue is the relationship between specific choices that teachers make about the use of allocated time and student achievement.

As previously noted, the most influential and widely cited study about the relationship of achievement to the allocation and use of time is the Beginning Teacher Evaluation Study (BTES). As a part of that study, a sample of students in the second grade and the fifth grade were administered a battery of achievement tests; they were observed one full day per week for 20 weeks by trained observers and their teachers kept a log of allocated time, per content category, for all school days between October and May. The project staff also gathered data on such activities as teacher planning functions and an assessment of general characteristics of the classroom and instructional program. Based on an analysis of the data, the BTES project researchers reported fourteen findings; five of those findings address the issue of the relationship of academic learning time and achievement. They are:

1. The amount of time that teachers allocate to instruction in a particular curriculum content area is positively associated with student learning in that content area.
2. The proportion of allocated time that students are engaged is positively associated with learning.
3. The proportion of time that reading or mathematics tasks are performed with high success (Academic Learning Time) is positively associated with student learning.
4. The proportion of time that reading or mathematics tasks are performed with low success is negatively associated with student learning.
5. Increases in Academic Learning Time are not associated with more negative attitudes toward mathematics, reading, or school.

BTES researchers concluded that Academic Learning Time is an important predictor of student achievement, and that Academic Learning Time can be interpreted as "an immediate, ongoing measure of student learning" (Fisher et al., 1980; Marliave, 1978).

Other researchers have also studied the way time is used in classrooms. At the elementary level, Cornbleth and Korth (1979) examined the relationship between subject area, day of the week, activity format, and previous student achievement growth in fourth-grade classrooms across four subject areas. They found differences in involved time for subject area, day of the week, and achievement growth. Gettinger and White (1979) also found a strong correlation between time to learn and achievement in several subject areas. At the secondary level, researchers have examined how time is used and the effects of such use at several grade levels and in multiple subject areas. Halasz and Behm (1983) assessed how time was used in three vocational education areas, providing baseline for further research in that field. Others have examined time on task in junior high and high school level mathematics (Seifert & Beck, 1983; Sanford & Evertson, 1982; Fitzgibbon & Clark, 1982; Probst, 1980); science (Deady, 1970; Burkman et al., 1981; Beasley, 1982; Dilleshaw & Okey, 1983); and physical education (Godbout et al., 1983).

In general, studies support a correlation between time on task and student achievement, although there appears to be variation by subject matter. For example, Sanford and Evertson (1982) found a significant relationship between time use and class achievement and attitude in junior high school mathematics classes, but not in English classes. They hypothesized that the reason for such a discrepancy is that there is more agreement and consistency about the content taught and appropriate instructional techniques in mathematics than in English, and that it is therefore possible to identify classroom-activity variables that contribute to mathematics learning. In the English classes that they studied, there was such a wide variation in goals and activities that the activity categories used in the study failed to describe some of the salient dimensions.

On the other hand, studies other than BTES which focus upon allotted time rather than engaged time show mixed results or no correlation with achievement. For example, Deady (1970) examined the effects of increased time allotments in science for fourth-grade students from 20 minutes/day to 35 minutes/day, and found no significant differences in achievement or attitude toward science that could be attributed either to time allotment or teacher preference for time allotment. Smith (1979) found that time allocated for social studies showed a very slight correlation with fifth graders' achievement, and suggested that allotted time should be carefully qualified when used as a variable in assessing instruction.

Several studies have considered the relationship of time on task to ability levels of students. Probst (1980) investigated differences occurring in time utilization by students of varying achievement levels in three mathematics teachers' classes, each of which varied in instructional mode, and found that high and middle achievers spent significantly more time on task than low achievers, and that in some cases there were significant differences in the level of time on task of students of similar ability levels in different classes. In an earlier study of time allotments by subjects in intermediate elementary grades, it was found that maximum period lengths resulted in greater achievement in every area tested for those with IQs of 115 or more; for those with lower IQ scores, longer periods resulted in significantly higher achievement only in the areas of mathematics and language (Jarvis, 1962). Good and Beckerman (1978) investigated whether pupil involvement in tasks was different for high, middle, and low achievers, and found that high achievers were more involved than low achievers, that there were different patterns of pupil involvement in different teachers' classrooms, and that the achievement gap became greater between high achievers and low achievers in the traditionally emphasized subjects.

Other studies have focused more specifically on the instructional techniques used in the classroom. Seifert and Beck (1983) found a positive correlation of both achievement gains and time on task with the lecture/ discussion strategy in algebra. Roadrangka & Yeany (1982) observed five student teachers, rating them according to instructional style (direct to indirect), quality of teaching strategies, developmental level, and time on task; they concluded that the type of strategy and the quality of the strategy have an influence on student time on task, and that there is a relationship between formal reasoning ability and time on task. Beasley (1982) observed 24 science teachers and categorized their instructional strategy into three types of instruction (exposition, exposition plus props, and demonstration); demonstration was used less frequently, but task involvement increased in the demonstration lesson segments.

The wide range of results of the studies cited above and others which examine factors related to time on task and achievement illustrate the difficulty of examining single or limited numbers of variables. A few studies, like BTES, have examined multiple variables. For example, Wilson et al. (1983) examined the effects of task arrangements and management systems on student engagement rates. They argue that the complexity of classroom arrangements influences the form and content of management systems, and that management decisions impact levels of student engagement. Such a position is congruent with Berliner's (1982) conception of the executive functions of teaching; like business executives, teachers must manage many complex tasks in a work setting in order to achieve the desired outcomes.

Time as a Mechanism for Studying other Topics

Time for learning is an important concept in itself, but it also has become a mechanism for studying other dimensions of the educational experience.

1. Collective Bargaining—Eberts and Pierce (1982) studied the possible effect of collective bargaining on time use. Based on a national survey of more than 3,000 elementary school teachers, they found that teachers covered by collective bargaining spent approximately three percent less time in instruction per day, or more than five days less in an 180 day school year. When related back to the Wiley-Harnischfeger model, this has potentially important achievement implications.

2. Bilingual Education—Ortiz (1980) studied a number of bilingual education projects, examining the proposals as well as observing in some projects. The proposals reflected relatively greater concern with staffing, materials, and teaching strategies and less with classroom management, teacher expectations and academic learning time. In at least one project, teacher-pupil interaction with bilingual students was reduced when bilingual aides were in the classroom. Teachers tended to initiate interaction with non-bilingual students; aides, with bilingual

students. This, and other practices, resulted in lower academic learning time for the bilingual students and seemed to lead to some classroom management problems.

3. Mainstreamed Children—Knowles (1982) conducted research on the academic learning time of handicapped and nonhandicapped students in mainstreamed elementary physical education classes. She found that both handicapped and nonhandicapped children had a significantly greater amount of academic learning time in individualized learning settings.

4. High and Low Achieving Children—Derevensky et al. (1981) found that high achieving inner city children spent significantly more time on task than did low achieving children; the time spent on learning was relatively high for both groups.

5. Minority and Disadvantaged Children—In a study of the opportunity given low income minority students to respond, Stanley and Greenwood (1983) learned that academic responding time was significantly lower among minority students in Title I schools. Gross (1983) reported four schools that were committed to raising achievement scores for disadvantaged students by increasing academic learning time.

6. Nontraditional Settings—Based upon data collected from observing twelve and thirteen year olds in a participatory museum exhibit, Falk (1983) concluded that time on task behavior provides a feasible basis for predicting learning.

7. Good and Poor Readers—Allington (1982) analyzed teacher logs for 600 elementary reading group sessions, and found that although teachers allocate the same amount of time for reading instruction for good and poor readers, the good readers are allowed to cover much more material in the same amount of time. Allotted time, while an appropriate initial measure of how time is distributed in the instructional program, does not indicate whether allocated time is actually used for its allocated purpose, or if it is, if it is used differentially among students.

Methodology and Criticism

Among the more perplexing aspects of research on academic learning time are those associated with observation methodology. Questions arise regarding how to decide whether a student is on or off task, which students should be sampled when observations are being made, how many students should be sampled, when observations should be made, and how long the observations should be. Although such questions have not been answered definitively, there are some useful preliminary results. The most systematic methodological study appears to have been one conducted by Karweit and Slavin (1981, 1982), in which they observed 18 second- to fifth-grade classrooms in a rural Maryland district. They considered the timing of observations, sampling of students and segments of instruction, and definitions of on-task behaviors. In this study, Karweit and Slavin found that altering the definition of time-on-task to classify momentary (less than one minute) off-task behaviors as being on-task, resulted both in classifying more behavior as being on-task and in slightly bettering the ability of on-task behavior to account for variation in posttest achievement test scores; however, the point that they make is not that there is increased ability to predict but that, because any methodological change could affect outcomes, all methodological decisions should be made on a rational rather than an arbitrary basis.

Karweit and Slavin also found that there is variation, by teacher, in the engagement rate for different ten-minute segments of a fifty-minute period. That is, where one teacher's engaged rate may be highest at the beginning of a class period, another one may peak during the third segment, and a third one, during the final segment. Furthermore, the higher the percent of the class period observed, the better was the prediction of achievement test scores.

Further analyses of their data by Karweit and Slavin revealed that both increased observation reliability and better prediction from the observations resulted as the number of fifty-minute observation periods was increased from five to nine to eighteen. On the other hand, there were only minor, nonsignificant differences between February (semester beginning) and May (semester ending) observations. Nor did reducing the number of students monitored from 12 to 6 make much difference. An even further reduction to three in number of students observed appeared to be tolerable if there were at least eight to ten observation periods. This study provides strong evidence of the care that must be taken in planning and conducting time-on-task observations for both classroom planning and research purposes.

Despite the generally positive response to the time for learning concept and its underlying research base, this relatively new field is not without its critics. Five kinds of criticism have been made: (1) the research methodology is inadequate (McNamara, 1981), (2) the relationships between time-on-task and achievement are too weak to justify modifying programs in an attempt to increase time-on-task (McNamara, 1981), (3) use of achievement tests as the primary outcome measure for education will bring an unfortunate narrowing of the curriculum (McNamara, 1981), (4) traditional methods texts and courses give a more sensitive and comprehensive treatment to issues related to attention (time-on-task) (McNamara, 1981; Confrey, 1982), and (5) there are problems in estimating time-on-task that are difficult to solve (Karweit & Slavin, 1982). McNamara (1981) is especially harsh in his analysis of the BTES methodology and what he considers inappropriately prescriptive procedures that various authors have projected from the data.

Implications for Practice

Despite the critics, there has been a considerable amount of interest in discovering ways in which the time on task concepts can be used for the improvement of education. The recommendations fall into three categories:

1. *School policies/leadership for effective use of time.* One of the consistent findings in studies of time utilization is that there is wide variation in the amount of the school day devoted to instruction, the amount of instructional time that is actually engaged time, and the amount of engaged time which is academic learning time. Many of the recommendations have therefore focused on increasing awareness of how time is used and planning for its more effective use. In the area of non-instructional time, schools have been encouraged to gather data and examine their policies on such time-related factors as length of the school year and school day; how time is scheduled within the school day; breaks, announcements, special events, and other potentially schedule-disrupting events; and program decisions such as the use of "pull-out" programs or special instructional programs for some children. The intent of such analyses should be to increase the amount of time which becomes available at the classroom level for instructional use (AASA, 1982; McREL, 1983). Stallings and Mohlman (1981), in a study of the impact of school policy on effective utilization of time, found that the role of the principal was critical; time-on-task improved and attitudes were more positive in schools where policies and rules were clear and consistent, where there was administrative support and fewer burdensome duties, and where the principal was collaborative, respectful, and supportive. Harnischfeger (1980), while supporting the position that research on issues such as time on task can make major contributions to policy development for school improvement, also expressed concern that policy issues typically enter the thinking of researchers only after the completion of a study rather than when the research problem and the design are being formulated. She recommends that policy issues be considered early in the definition of a research or development effort.

2. *Analysis of time on task in the classroom.* A second category of recommendations in the time on task literature focuses on how effectively that time is used. When academic learning time is considered, recommendations shift from the time on task research to a broader research base which includes alternative models of learning, assumptions about curricular and instructional goals and values, and research on classroom management. (See papers by Stallings and Bruning, this volume.)

DISCUSSION

The Beginning Teacher Evaluation study and the related research by Carroll, Harnischfeger and Wiley, Evertson and Sanford and others have generated a high level of interest in the issue of time utilization and how such utilization affects student achievement. Perhaps the most important contribution that such research has made is that it has caused educators to think about what happens in schools in a new way; time is now seen as a variable which can be manipulated rather than as a "given," part of the general context in which schools operate.

At the same time, there is some concern that the findings of BTES and the related studies will be treated as prescriptions rather than as a broad descriptive base that educators can use to analyze their own classrooms and schools and make decisions about curriculum and instruction. Several researchers have offered cautions about the data base, the assumptions, and the generalizability of the data produced thus far, and express the fear that time on task may be treated as a simplistic notion, rather than as a complex phenomenon which warrants careful interpretation before application.

How might the research on time on task be useful to the individual classroom teacher or to a school? For the teacher, the research provides both a methodology and a construct for understanding what is taking place in his or her classroom. The data generated by keeping logs of time allocation and conducting time on task "audits" of individual students in different subject areas and instructional activities can serve as one tool to assist teachers in understanding the consequences of current practice and to adapt their instruction, if desired. For school building staffs or for school districts, the time on task concept and instruments can be a means of generating data for policy formulation and guidelines about how time is allocated, and what kinds of activities may cut into the time allocated for instruction.

It may be important, however, to be aware of the ways in which the time on task concepts and data gathering techniques should *not* be used. Time on task is not a prescriptive device, and there is no simple "right" level of allocated learning time that should be present in every classroom. It might be very tempting for teachers or administrators to assume that more is always better, and to focus on counting time on task rates rather than the interrelationship between time utilization and instructional goals and alternative strategies. Time-on-task is also not an evaluation tool, and should not be used as a means of rating teachers.

How might the time on task research be useful to teacher educators as they prepare teachers? There are several concepts both explicit and implicit within that body of research which preservice teachers need to understand. First, a teacher has only a finite block of time within which to teach. Prospective teachers need to understand how time gets subtracted from that initial block of time, through such factors as absences, "snow days," interruptions from announcements and loudspeakers, the need for discipline, and other intrusions. They also need to realize how time becomes lost within the instructional process, to understand ways in which time is used profitably, and to know how they can make decisions which will increase the amount of learning time in their classrooms.

There needs to be explicitness in presenting these concepts to preservice teachers; they need concrete descriptions, as much detail as possible, and opportunities to use the concepts in practical settings. At the same time, teacher educators, like the school personnel, need to be careful that the time on task research does not get used prescriptively by preservice teachers. There is a great temptation to "count minutes" and equate on-task as good and off-task as bad. As several of the studies cited have shown, some off-task time is both necessary and inevitable.

Time-on-task research must be integrated with other forms of research in teacher education programs. In this document there are six papers on specific research topics, of which this paper is one. Each of the other topics has a relationship to time on task. The literature on classroom management, for example, must be considered when one is making decisions about the use of time. (See paper by Vasa, this volume.) If a teacher has decided that although she knows the highest attention rate is usually found in teacher-led presentations and that lower attention rates usually occur during seatwork, she still wants to use seatwork because of a particular goal, she may benefit from the advice that the management literature gives her on assigning seatwork, giving directions, and managing transitions. As another example, a teacher who understands the developmental characteristics of students may make different choices about time allocation and instructional strategies than one who has not considered the two bodies of research in relationship to each other. (See paper by Santmire and Friesen, this volume.)

References

Allington, R. L. (1982, November). *Content coverage and contextual reading in reading groups.* Paper presented at annual meeting of the National Council of Teachers of English, 72nd, Washington, DC. ED 228 604.

Beasley, W. (1982, September). Teacher demonstrations: The effect on student task involvement. *Journal of Chemical Education, 59*(9), 789-90.

Berliner, D. C. (1982). The executive functions of teaching. Paper presented at the meeting of the American Educational Research Association, New York City.

Bruning, R. H. (1984). Key elements of effective teaching in the direct teaching model. (This volume.)

Burkman, E., & others. (1981, November). Effects of academic ability, time allowed for study, and teacher directedness on achievement in a high school science course (ISIS). *Journal of Research in Science Teaching, 18*(6), 563-76.

Carroll, J. B. (1963). A model of school learning. *Teachers College Record, 64*, 723-33.

Coleman, J. S., & others. (1966). *Equality of educational opportunity.* Washington, DC: Government Printing Office.

Confrey, J. (1982). Review of "time to learn" subject-matter specialists. *Journal of Classroom Interaction, 17(2)*, 32-36.

Cornbleth, C., & Korth, W. (1979, April). *Instructional, context, and individual differences in pupil involvement in learning activity.* Paper presented at the annual meeting of the American Educational Research Association, San Francisco, CA. ED 171 409.

Daniels, A. F., & Haller, E. J. (1981). Exposure to instruction, surplus time, and student achievement: A local replication of the Harnischfeger and Wiley research. *Educational Administration Quarterly, 17(1)*, 48-68.

Deady, G. M. (1970, March). *The effects of an increased time allotment on student attitudes and achievement in science.* Paper presented at annual meeting of the National Association for Research in Science Teaching, 43rd, Minneapolis, MN. ED 039 126.

Derevensky, J. L., & others. (1981). *An examination of achievement related behavior of high and low achieving inner city pupils.* Paper presented at the annual convention of the American Educational Research Association, Los Angeles, CA.

DeVault, M. L., & others. (1977). *Schooling and learning opportunity, interim report.* St. Ann, MO: Central Midwestern Regional Lab.

Dilleshaw, F. G., & Okey, J. R. (1983). Effects of a modified mastery learning strategy on achievement, attitudes, and on-task behavior of high school chemistry students. *Journal of Research in Science Teaching, 20(3)*, 203-11.

Eberts, R. W., & Pierce, L. C. (1982). *Time in the classroom: The effect of collective bargaining on the allocation of teacher time.* Eugene, OR: Center for Educational Policy and Management.

Falk, J. H. (1983). Time and behavior as predictors of learning. *Science Education, 67(2)*, 267-76.

Fisher, C. W., & others. (1980). Teaching behaviors, academic learning time, and student achievement: An overview. In C. Denham & A. Lieberman (Eds.), *Time to learn* (pp. 7-32). Washington, DC: Government Printing Office.

Fitzgibbon, C. T., & Clark, K. S. (1982, November). Time variables in classroom research: A study of eight urban secondary school mathematics classes. *British Journal of Educational Psychology, 52(3)*, 301-16.

Forlano, G. (1936). School learning with various methods of practice and rewards. *Teachers College Contributions to Education, No. 688.*

Frandsen, A. (1957). *How children learn: An educational psychology.* New York: McGraw-Hill.

Gettinger, M., & White, M. A. (1979, August). Which is the stronger correlate of school learning? Time to learn or measured intelligence? *Journal of Educational Psychology, 71(4)*, 405-12.

Godbout, P., & others. (1983, March). Academic learning time in elementary and secondary physical education classes. *Research Quarterly for Exercise and Sport, 54*(1), 11-19.

Good, T. L., & Beckerman, T. M. (1978, January). Time on task: A naturalistic study in sixth-grade classrooms. *Elementary School Journal, 78*(3), 192-201.

Gross, B. (1983). Can compensatory education produce higher achievement with reduced resources? *Educational Leadership, 40*(5), 44-47.

Halasz, I. M., & Behm, K. S. (1983, January). Time on task in selected vocational education classes. Columbus, OH: Ohio State University, National Center for Research in Vocational Education. ED 229 528.

Harnischfeger, A. (1980). Curricular control and learning time: District policy, teacher strategy, and pupil choice. *Educational Evaluation and Policy Analysis, 2*(6), 19-30.

Harnischfeger, A., & Wiley, D. E. (1976). The teaching-learning process in elementary schools: A synoptic view. *Curriculum Inquiry, 6*(1), 5-43.

Jarvis, Oscar T. (1962, November). Time allotments and pupil achievement in the intermediate elementary grades. A Texas Gulf Coast study. Houston University, Texas, Bureau of Educational Research and Service. ED 035 063.

Karweit, N., & Slavin, R. E. (1981). Measurement and modeling choices in studies of time and learning. *American Educational Research Journal, 18*(2), 157-71.

Karweit, N., & Slavin, R. E. (1982). Time-on-task issues of timing, sampling, and definition. *Journal of Educational Psychology, 74*(6), 844-51.

Knowles, C. J., & others. (1982). Relationship of individualized teaching strategies to academic learning time for mainstreamed handicapped and non-handicapped students. *Journal of Special Education, 16*(4), 449-56.

Mann, C. H. (1928). *How schools use their time: Practice in 444 cities including a study of trends from 1826 to 1926.* New York: Teachers College, Columbia University.

Marliave, R. (1978, March). *Academic learning time and achievement: The validation of a measure of ongoing student engagement and task difficulty.* Paper presented at the annual meeting of the American Educational Research Association, 62nd, Toronto, Ontario, Canada. ED 160 661.

McGeoch, J. A. (1942). *The psychology of human learning.* New York: Longmans, Green.

McNamara, D. R. (1981). Attention, time-on-task and children's learning: Research or ideology? *Journal of Education for Teaching, 7*(3), 284-97.

McREL. (1983). Mimeographed materials prepared for the cooperative mid-Nebraska schools/UN-L project.

National Commission on Excellence in Education. *A nation at risk.* Washington, DC: U.S. Department of Education.

Ortiz, F. I. (1980). *Significant instructional features in bilingual education.* Paper presented at the American Educational Research Association convention, Boston, MA.

Powell, M. (1980). The beginning teacher evaluation study: A brief history of a major research project. In C. Denham & A. Lieberman (Eds.), *Time to learn* (pp. 1-5). Washington, DC: Government Printing Office.

Probst, D. (1980, November). *A study of time-on-task in three teachers' classrooms using different instructional modes.* Report from the project on studies of instructional programming for the individual student. Madison: Wisconsin University. Research and Development Center for Individualized Schooling. ED 196 905.

Roadrangka, V., & Yeany, R. H. (1982, April). *A study of the relationship among type and quality of implementation of science and teaching strategy, student formal reasoning ability, and student engagement.* Paper presented at the National Conference of the Association for the Education of Teachers in Science, Chicago, IL. ED 215 896.

Rosenshine, B. (1980). How time is spent in elementary classrooms. In C. Denham & A. Lieberman (Eds.), *Time to learn* (pp. 107-26). Washington, DC: Government Printing Office.

Sanford, J. P., & Evertson, C. M. (1982). Time use and activities in junior high classes. *Journal of Educational Research, 76(3),* 140-47.

Santmire, T. E., & Friesen, P. A. (1984). A developmental analysis of research on effective teacher-student interactions: Implications for teacher preparation. (This volume.)

Seifert, E. H., & Beck, J. J. (1983, March). Time/learning relationships in secondary schools: A research report. ED 229 853.

Smith, N. M. (1979, March-April). Allocation of time and achievement in elementary social studies. *Journal of Educational Research, 72(4),* 231-36.

Squires, D. A., Huitt, W. G., & Segars, J. K. (1983). *Effective schools and classrooms: A research-based perspective.* Association for Supervision and Curriculum Development; Arlington, VA.

Stallings, J. (1980). Allocated academic learning time revisited, or beyond time on task. *Educational Researcher, 9(11),* 11-16.

Stallings, J. (1984). Implications from the research on teaching for teacher preparation. (This volume.)

Stallings, J., & Mohlman, G. G. (1981, September). *School policy, leadership style, teacher change and student behavior in eight schools, Final report.* Mountain View, CA: Stallings Teaching and Learning Institute. ED 209 759.

Stanley, S. O., & Greenwood, C. R. (1983). How much opportunity to respond does the minority disadvantaged student receive in school? *Exceptional Children, 49(4),* 370-73.

Thorndike, E. L. (1931). *Human learning.* New York: Appleton-Century.

Time on task. (1982). Arlington, VA: American Association of School Administrators.

Vasa, S. F. (1984). Classroom management: A selected review of the literature. (This volume.)

Wiley, D. E., & Harnischfeger, A. (1974). Explosion of a myth: Quantity of schooling and exposure to instruction, major educational vehicles. *Educational Researcher, 3(4)*, 7-12.

Wilson, B. L., & others. (1983, April). *Effect of task and authority structures on student task engagement.* Paper presented at the annual meeting of the American Educational Research Association, Montreal, Quebec, Canada. ED 230 416.

Models of Teaching
And Teacher Education

Alvah M. Kilgore
University of Nebraska-Lincoln

Thc term "models of teaching" was used by Joyce and Weil (1972, 1980) as the title of a book about teaching. The authors defined a teaching model as a sequence of teaching skills or acts that are used to achieve predetermined objectives or ends, and usually are based upon the seminal work of a major psychologist or theorist, such as Skinner, Brunner or Taba. However, a few models were generated from the academic disciplines (e.g., the B.S.C.S. science inquiry model), and some were developed by researchers who observed teaching practices that seemed to work (e.g., Glasser's Classroom Meeting model or Roger's Non-directive Teaching model).

Teaching models differ from what we generally refer to as "methods" in the sense that methods of teaching are more general than are models of teaching. For example, the lecture method generally refers to didactic large group instruction where the teacher does all of the talking. A model of teaching, on the other hand, might encompass an oral presentation of one form or another (Kilgore, 1977), or the use of Advance Organizers (Ausubel, 1963), each of which might be subsumed under the general label of lecturing, a teaching method. Another example of this difference between teaching methods and models might begin with the general teaching method called inquiry. Teaching models subsumed under this label could include the Jurisprudential model (Oliver and Shaver, 1971), Inquiry Training (Suchman, 1962), or the Group Investigation Model developed by Thelan (1960).

A teaching model, then, is a distinct set of ordered steps or phases created to achieve certain outcomes. These outcomes are different for different models, although some similarities exist among certain models, thus permitting the formation of model "clusters." Joyce and Weil (1980) classified and labeled several clusters of models into larger groupings which they termed "families" (see Appendix A). Through such a structure of teaching models, educational researchers and practitioners are able to study models of teaching singularly, within families, or between families. They also can make teaching decisions as to what family, and model within a family, would be best suited to achieve an outcome desired by a teacher. In a sense, Joyce and Weil have done for teaching what Bloom has done for cognitive and affective levels of thinking. They have provided an organizational context and taxonomy for looking at different kinds of teaching, providing alternatives for teacher educators as well as teachers, and also providing a base for studying teaching patterns that heretofore have been somewhat elusive. Additionally, models of teaching can be used to shape curriculum in both a short and long term way, to aid in designing instructional materials and to guide instruction in the classroom.

Weil and Murphy (1982) wrote that research results have demonstrated that instructional processes make a significant contribution to student outcomes. Furthermore, different instruction processes appear to promote goals associated with those particular processes. Thus, instructional processes are generally designed to accomplish distinct objectives. Some researchers have not noted these differences and consequently have conducted studies which compared cereal and beefsteak rather than two kinds of beefsteak. This practice has led to ill-designed research. For example, the much maligned lecture method of teaching has often been used as a comparison method for inquiry types of teaching methodologies. Those doing the comparing were seeking to show that the inquiry method was better than the lecture method, but they did not take into account that the purposes, intended outcomes, and appropriate methods for measuring results of these methods were strikingly different.

Through the years, teaching models have become more theoretically based and delineated into clearly describable patterns of teacher behavior. This has facilitated the work of researchers documenting the contribution of teaching strategies (models) to educational outcomes. For instance, many of the isolated behaviors identified as part of the direct instruction repertoire of effective teachers have been more powerfully characterized by describing them in terms of a teaching model or strategy.

As mentioned above, Joyce and Weil (1980) organized different models of teaching into four families, which have been described more fully by Weil and Murphy (1982). The *Information Processing Family* of models addresses the ways students can improve their ability to master information, including capacities to organize data, generate concepts, solve problems, and use verbal and nonverbal symbols. The *Personal Family* of models addresses development of unique, individual realities, with attention to development of emotional life. The *Social Interaction Family* emphasizes the relationship of the individual to society or to other persons and seeks to improve one's ability to relate to others and to engage in the democratic process. The *Behavioral Family* shares a common theoretical base variously referred to as "learning theory," "social learning theory," and "behavior therapy." These models address a wide variety of goals but always with emphasis on changing behavior from less productive to more productive patterns.

When creating the concepts and models found in *Models of Teaching*,

Joyce and Weil became convinced that there was not a "right" way to teach. Rather, there were many "right" teaching strategies available for teachers to use in trying to teach the variety of students that one normally finds in a classroom. One might recall that during the 1960's and early 1970's each of several developers of teaching programs suggested that he or she had a monopoly on how to teach. Among the strategies developed were the Hilda Taba Teaching Strategies Program, Individually Prescribed Instruction (IPI), Individually Guided Education (IGE), and Man: A Course of Study, a curriculum that was based on a particular teaching strategy. Each of these programs, and the behaviors that were espoused for teachers within the program, could be construed as a model of teaching.

Joyce and Weil's position (1972) is that " . . . we should not limit our methods to any single model, however attractive that model may seem at first glance, because no model of teaching is designed to accomplish all types of learning or to work for all learning styles" (p.1). Rather, a teacher must acquire a "repertoire" of teaching skills, strategies and models, and know how and when to use them in a multitude of teaching situations in much the same way that a doctor must be able to call upon a variety of medicines and treatments to cure a patient or an engineer must use a variety of skills to design and build a bridge. This concept seems especially valid if one takes into consideration the research on learning styles, limited as it is at this time. Additionally, teachers continue to teach groups (classes) of children rather than individuals, and grouping policies and practices generally do not reflect learning styles as much as they do reading ability.

This paper is organized around (a) five models of teaching, drawn from two of the Joyce and Weil families, with the discussion of each model having both a description and an indication of the model's probable impact, and (b) the relationship of models of teaching to a teacher education program.

Selected Models of Teaching

Several models of teaching have been more heavily researched than others. Five of those models are described in this paper. A sixth model that has a comprehensive research base, direct teaching is discussed by Bruning in this monograph. (See paper by Bruning, this volume.) In addition, in this monograph, Santmire discusses the applications of research done by Piaget and other developmentalists in rationalizing the use of different instructional strategies with children and youth at differing stages of development. Although based on much the same research foundation as Joyce and Weil's "Cognitive Development" model, which they classify as a member of the Information Processing Family, Santmire's discussion is somewhat more inclusive than a single model.

Three other models from the Information Processing Family have also been rather comprehensively researched. They are: *The Advance Organizer* model, (Ausubel, 1963); *The Inductive Thinking* model (Taba, 1966); and the *Concept Attainment* model (Bruner, 1966). Two additional models from the

Behavioral Family also have an extensive research base. Both of these flow from the work of Skinner (1953). They are the *Contingency Management* model (behavior modification) and the *Self Management* strategy. These five models with their research bases, are those that are described and analyzed in this paper.

The Advance Organizer Model

Developed by David Ausubel (1963, 1968), this model is of interest to teacher educators for three reasons: first, it is one of the most heavily researched of all teaching strategies; second, it is relatively easy to learn yet has great impact; and third, it has general applicability for it uses the lecture and recitation aspects of teaching behaviors as a base. Ausubel's theory centers on the idea that organizers should be introduced in advance of new learning tasks and should be formulated so that they take into account ideas and concepts already existing in the cognitive structure of the learner. Ausubel defines advance organizers

> . . . as introductory material at a higher level of abstraction, generality, and inclusiveness than the learning passage itself, and an overview as a summary presentation of the principal ideas in a passage that is not necessarily written at a higher level of abstraction, generality, and inclusiveness, but achieves its effect largely by the simple omission of specific detail" (Ausubel, 1978, p. 251).

The Advance Organizer model does not purport to apply to all school learning, such as rote learning, motor skills, perceptual learning, concept formation, thinking or problem solving. Ausubel asserts, however, that his model covers the *major* cognitive learning activities that take place in school, the kind of learning that constitutes the primary objective of the school as a social institution and that is the efficient and meaningful transmission of the important subject matter disciplines. The model is based on research and theory of how humans learn and *retain* large bodies of subject matter in classrooms. The theory is limited to reception learning and retention, i.e., learning that includes the notion of the content (what is to be learned) as being *presented* to the learner rather than having the learner independently discover the same material.

The material to be learned, the content, appears to be as important to the use of this model as the model itself. Ausubel wrote that generally all subject areas are developed in a hierarchy of concepts and relationships between concepts. The role of a teacher is to know the subject area and its structure along with the students' level of knowledge about the content to be learned, and to create an advance organizer lesson using both of these factors. If teachers provide students with advance organizers, the new material to be learned and time to integrate the new material into previously learned structures, students will retain and use these data to a significantly higher degree than will students of teachers who do not use advance organizers.

Ausubel's research has shown a consistent 12 to 20 percent increase in gain scores for students of teachers using this model (Ausubel, 1978). Other researchers following Ausubel's lead have reported gain scores up to 50 percent higher for students taught using the model (Lawton and Wanska, 1977).

Ausubel's work has not gone uncriticized. Barnes and Clawson (1975), based on a review of 32 studies on the uses of advance organizers, concluded that their efficacy had not been established. In responding to the Barnes and Clawson critique, Lawton and Wanska (1977) indicated that the critique of the advance organizer strategy was based on poor information and interpretation of data on the part of Barnes and Clawson, but that Ausubel's work did need additional investigation. More specifically, Lawton and Wanska suggested that (1) techniques should be developed for identifying and constructing organizers for particular types of learning, (2) the relationship between the concept of advance organizers and associated expository teaching techniques and learning activities needs further refinement, and (3) several stages and factors need to be considered in developing and evaluating advance organizers. Ausubel (1978), in turn, accused his critics of superficiality in their review methodology as well as a gross misinterpretation of "operational definition" in their criticism of his definition of advance organizers. He cited several recent studies in which teachers used advance organizers as intended. The results indicated that subject matter was learned more effectively by more types of learners, a more complete understanding of the subject area was accomplished, children's cognitive movement was facilitated from preoperational to concrete operational, and that there were increases in mean learning scores. From the evidence presented by Ausubel and others, it appears that advance organizers, when used with the expository method, constitute a viable teaching model that can be learned by pre- and in-service teachers and that this model should become part of a teachers' repertoire of teaching skills.

The Inductive Thinking Model

Taba (1966), in synthesizing the available research on thinking, thinking styles and strategies, concluded that a new teaching strategy and a new role for the teacher had emerged, which was to stimulate cognitive processes in children. In order to accomplish this role effectively, teachers had to have a "cognitive map" of the concepts and mental operations involved in the various learning tasks to be able to diagnose the type and the level of thought processes children bring to the tasks. When Taba reviewed the research on teaching available at that time, she concluded that, with training, teachers could be taught how to develop thinking skills in students. From this base she developed a series of teaching strategies that, when employed by a teacher, should have a variety of useful effects on students. These effects, in varying degrees, would include (1) use of higher level thinking skills, (2) better retention and use of factual information, and (3) increased ability of students to use this information in the form of concepts and generalizations. Taba thought that use of these strategies also would lead to better self images as well as improved interactive skills.

The specific teaching strategies developed by Taba, and labeled as the

112

Inductive Teaching Model by Joyce and Weil, were the tasks of concept formation, inferring and generalizing, and the application of principles. Each of these tasks could be viewed as a separate teaching model, for each can be operated independently and each can be taught to teachers as a separate strategy.

Taba also constructed a curriculum which included the use of these tasks as a part of the behavior required by a teacher. Using students and teachers at the elementary level, an experimental research program was conducted to test the efficacy of her theory. The experimental design included organizing a new curriculum plus training teachers to develop cognitive processes in their students. The study had a single target, the development of cognitive processes (thinking skills) in children. The study examined the relationship of the target objective to: student content achievement, intelligence, economic status and reading and language ability. In the process, the functions of the individual teacher acts and of the combinations of these acts were also studied. Taba reached two major conclusions based on this study. First, thinking levels of children could be raised with the application of the stimuli put forth by the teacher and the material to be studied. Second, teachers could be taught to use these teaching strategies in their classrooms.

After Taba's death in 1969, her work was carried on by several of her students and colleagues. One such program, titled the *Hilda Taba Teaching Strategies Program* and sponsored by the Institute for Staff Development, became a widespread effort involving several cities and states in training teachers to utilize the teaching models developed by Taba.

Another contribution from Taba concerned considerations teachers use when making decisions about teaching. Taba originally was a curriculum worker. She began her studies of teaching when she observed few operational relationships between curriculum development and what occurred in classrooms and concluded that something needed to be developed to help bridge the gap between teaching and the curriculum being taught. She wrote that decisions regarding teaching strategies are affected first by the nature of the content taught and second by one's view of that content.

The Concept Attainment Model

The study of concepts and conceptual thinking has a rich history in psychology dating back to the original studies by Hull (1920). More recently, Bruner's contributions have been critical. They are twofold. First, his seminal work on concept attainment was published in *A Study of Thinking* (1956) and provided the basis for his second contribution, his follow-up work on the teaching of concepts.

The development of concepts is primarily a categorization process. In order to think, people need to categorize. There are primarily two ways to categorize, perceptually and conceptually. Perceptual categorization is an immediate phenomenon, accomplished primarily through visual stimuli. As an object is observed, it is generally placed into some category of similar objects. Conceptual categorization is harder to define and identify, for the use of a

113

particular concept requires a specific experiential background. That is, the observer must be able to compare or relate the new phenomenon with past experiences or concepts. Bruner et al. (1966) provided the rationale for the importance of categorization by writing that categorization (1) reduces the complexity of the environment, (2) is the means by which the objects in the world about us are identified, and (3) reduces the necessity of constant learning. The concept attainment activity, then, is the process of finding predictive and defining attributes that distinguish exemplars from nonexemplars of the concept one seeks to attain.

Results of the research on concept attainment indicated that (1) concept attainment strategies and shifts in strategies can be located and described; (2) people, when categorizing or identifying exemplars from nonexemplars, especially with something new, will fall back to cues that worked in the past, whether the exemplars seem to fit the situation or not; (3) people are generally not willing to use nonexemplars of the concept to help them delimit the correct concept because this task calls for a transfer of thinking and people generally would rather not work with such transfers to help them make a decision. Additional findings indicated that subjects in the studies were flexible, that is, they could jump to conclusions when forced to under pressures of time or limited exemplars, and that subjects always seemed to try to reduce the exemplars to simpler, more easily ascertained cues. Finally, people could not generally describe how they arrived at a concept; they appeared to just "muddle" through (Bruner et al., 1956).

These early findings were important because it was from them that Bruner and his associates developed the model of teaching titled Concept Attainment (Bruner et al., 1977). In order to teach different types of concepts to different types and ages of learners, Bruner et al. (1977) developed three variations for Concept Attainment. In the first variation, exemplars are provided to students; these exemplars are labeled as exemplars or nonexemplars of the concept. This is called the reception mode. In this mode, the teacher's role is to help students see the relationship between exemplars as well as understand why nonexemplars are not a part of the concept being sought. Like Taba, Bruner indicated that the teacher must have a full understanding of the concept being sought in order to help students attain the concept. The second variation in concept attainment has been labeled the selection mode. In this mode, students are presented with a group of unlabeled exemplars and they ask questions about the various exemplars. The teacher provides the category (exemplar or nonexemplar) and students then generate and test their hypotheses. The third, and most difficult mode, is the unorganized materials mode. During this activity, students view the material presented by the teacher, locate and label the concept, and then identify additional exemplars for the concept. Each of Bruner's three modes of concept attainment is concluded by having the students identify the thinking processes used to arrive at the concept. This is especially important because as students learn how to categorize more effectively and as they learn how they arrived at their categories, their ability to attain concepts increases.

The concept attainment model may be used with all ages and grade levels. It allows a teacher to teach concepts which are both the key building blocks of instructional materials and the main element of a learner's cognitive structure. The model not only can be used to introduce extended series of inquiries into important areas, but also can support ongoing inductive study where the learning of concepts is important. Finally, use of the model has been found to be an excellent motivator, for students can become excited about studying when they are contributing to the attainment of the concept under study.

The Contingency Management Model

The Contingency Management Model, and the model to follow (The Self-Management Strategy), both flow from the work of B. F. Skinner. In his book, *Science and Human Behavior*, Skinner (1953) outlined his premises and rules for operant conditioning and explained the research leading to his conclusions and rules. It was from these basic notions that behaviorist research for the next two decades was conducted and from which most of the behaviorist practices currently in classroom use evolved. Operant conditioning is based on carefully programming the consequences following a given response and relies heavily on principles of reinforcement. Since the publication of *Science and Human Behavior*, there has been an immense amount of research and writing conducted concerning various phases, structures and uses of behaviorism. The most extensive use of these principles in education can be found in special education classes and in classroom management practices (Becker, Engelmann & Thomas, 1975a). A teacher, for instance, can improve classroom management by learning how to reinforce students for appropriate instead of inappropriate behavior. The Contingency Management Model relies mostly on the principles of operant conditioning, particularly reinforcement practices. Practices associated with this model in schools include the systematic control of reinforcers so that they are presented at selected times and only after the desired response has been given. A positive reinforcer increases the probability that the desired behavior will be repeated. If reinforcement activities are not used after a given behavior, the behavior may soon disappear.

Reinforcers can be positive or negative. Both work to a degree; however, positive reinforcers (e.g., smiles, praise, touches, tokens) work more effectively than do negative reinforcers (e.g., yelling, nagging and threatening). Negative reinforcers, sometimes called punishment, frequently create undesirable side effects such as disliking school and/or teacher or developing a poor self-image. Contingency management emphasizes positive reinforcement and specifically discourages the use of negative stimuli.

Three types of positive reinforcers are used most commonly in schools. The first type of reinforcer is social in nature, such as a hug, approval, a smile, attention. Social reinforcers work effectively with young children. A second type of reinforcer is material in nature, e.g., tokens, candy, toys, stars on a chart after one's name, displays of students' work, etc. The last group of reinforcers is labeled activity reinforcers and generally refer to promising participants the opportunity to engage in a more desirable activity once the initial activity is successfully completed. An example of this type of reinforcer was described in a mastery learning situation whereby students could leave school for a day upon successful completion of a unit of work. The data from researchers concerning the types and uses of reinforcers is not consistent; however, a combined application of several reinforcers may be more effective in increasing desirable behavior and in reducing deviant behavior than any single reinforcer (Becker, Engelmann & Thomas, 1971).

Another area in which contingency management practices appear to work well is in programmed instruction. Learning units are constructed so that students can achieve a high degree of success, materials are carefully presented in small, sequential steps, and immediate feedback is given as to correctness of the student's response. Programmed instruction is most often developed for individual students; however, there are programs available for small groups of students who have been diagnosed as being at about the same level (e.g., Becker, Engelmann & Thomas, 1975b).

There is a great deal of material and research concerning the use of the contingency management model of teaching. The following procedures were derived from the research for organizing the learning environment when using the model: (1) specifying the final performance desired; (2) assessing entering behavior (diagnosing); (3) formulating a contingency management program or plan; (4) instituting the program; and (5) evaluating the program (Joyce & Weil, 1980). Joyce and Weil also offered a cautionary note with respect to the expectations for using the model. They wrote that even with the impressive and well-documented history of the model, with many facets of learning and many types of learners, " . . . reinforcement is not effective all the time with every student. Certain elements contribute to the success of reinforcement" (p. 343). For example, young children respond more to social reinforcers; the nature of the reinforcer is a factor; people have different personality styles, and contingency management principles may work better with some learning styles.

The Self-Control Model

The principles of operant conditioning as described by Skinner (1953) and utilized so effectively in the Contingency Management Model are also applicable in the Self-Control Model. The major difference is that the reinforcement responsibilities are under the control of the participant. Part of the rationale for moving toward self-control as a teaching model is that for many behaviors the school environment is unlikely to provide incentives at the rate and time that an individual might need them in order to establish a new behavior.

The activities of the self-control model are similar to contingency management; the major difference is that students are made aware of the process and, as much as possible, given responsibility for decisionmaking. The research on self-management suggests that there should be a gradual phasing in of student responsibility for decisionmaking. The major phases of the model include: (1) providing the student with an introduction to behavior principles and skills; (2) establishing baseline data about the target behavior (e.g., establishing weight if going on a weight loss or gain program), and teaching the procedures for self assessment; (3) setting up the contingency program, which may include self-administration of contingencies, self-determination of contingencies, and self-instruction techniques; (4) implementing and modifying the self-management program; and (5) withdrawal of contingencies. It is important to note that self-control processes must be taught, not just told to the students (Joyce & Weil, 1980).

Research on
Learning the Models of Teaching

A basic premise of the use of *Models of Teaching* is that there is not a single best way to teach and that process-product research has not identified many generic teaching behaviors. This inability of finding substantive generic teaching behaviors has puzzled researchers even though a few teaching behaviors and practices such as clarity, variability of discourse, and enthusiasm, (Rosenshine & Furst, 1971) and time-on-task (Stallings, 1983) have been identified positively with increased pupil learning. Joyce (1981) and the models of teaching researchers hypothesized that teachers teach in patterns of behaviors, that is, clusters and sequences of activities rather than concentrating on specific, single teaching skills, and that if specific teaching behaviors were used it would be in combination with other skills. They further speculated that teaching sequences could be learned, and if teachers were to develop a "repertoire" of teaching models and skills that outcomes in terms of student learning could be measured. These notions were supported by theorists such as Eisner (1983) who referred to the teacher as an artist who orchestrated the content to be learned, knowledge of the learners and the ability to perform several teaching skills into an artistic whole; and researchers such as Gage (1979) who referred to the modern teacher as having to develop and utilize the "science of the art of teaching."

One of the early studies on the use of teaching models utilized twenty-six post baccalaureate students who were exposed to three models of teaching throughout a year-long training program. The primary research question asked was whether it was possible to use instructional systems to teach a repertoire of teaching models to a sufficient degree that the trainee could actualize them in a classroom. Results indicated that the trainees did shift their patterns of verbal interaction with students in the directions specified by the models. When compared with the teaching style of the cooperating teacher (who was not trained in models of teaching), the trainee's non-model teaching style was somewhat related to the cooperating teacher's style, but the model practice behavior was not related to the model of the cooperating teacher. Few cooperating teachers exhibited the behaviors that were critical to the models of teaching. The teacher trainees had to introduce new patterns of teaching into the classrooms if they were to implement the models they had learned (Seperson & Joyce, 1973). Another result from the study related to conceptual level theory (Harvey, Hunt & Shroder, 1961). Conceptual theory would indicate that one's ability to conceptualize at an abstract level would allow one to learn and utilize a variety of information, in this instance, a number of teaching models. Participants did learn to utilize three models of teaching in addition to their predetermined teaching style and also those behaviors practiced by the cooperating teachers. It was thought that conceptual levels could be changed by the increased use of teaching models (Joyce, Wald & Weil, 1981).

Research has been conducted to determine the possibility of training teachers in the Taba models. One such study utilizing 2000 teachers in San Diego reported modest gains in both teacher behaviors and attitudes toward teaching as a result of participating in a year-long inservice program centered around the teaching models developed by Taba (Stickel, 1972). Another study indicated that preservice students could be taught to use the Taba models in micro-teaching and field-based situations, provided support systems were available for the students (Kilgore, 1977).

Additional research on learning a repertoire of teaching models was conducted by Joyce and Showers (1981) and Showers (1983). Results from these studies indicated that a teacher's familiarity with the recommended teaching practices (how foreign they are to the teacher's existing repertoire) may be an important factor influencing the choice of training activities. Teachers who were less familiar with the models learned in workshops tended to need additional training activities after presentation and demonstration (Joyce & Showers, 1982). It was also found that a teacher's conceptual level was positively related to transfer of training among coached teachers; more abstract thinkers were more capable of using the recommended models of teaching as intended. Among uncoached teachers, no relationships were found between conceptual level and ability to use a specific teaching model. Training that was most effective included theory, demonstration, practice, feedback, and classroom application (Showers, 1983). In these studies, coaching referred to the practice of having trainers visit with and observe trainees as they practiced the newly acquired teaching models in their classrooms and provide feedback on skill development and model use. It would appear that the same principles could be applied to undergraduate teacher trainees within their methods courses and field experiences.

A synthesis of the research on preparing preservice students to use models of teaching found that, as with practicing teachers, the higher the conceptual level of a preservice student, the greater the teaching repertoire he or she could learn. Inservice teachers could learn models of teaching at a faster rate than preservice students, could recall and utilize the models more effectively when asked, but would not use models in a regular teaching situation unless the training program had the coaching element built in (Joyce & Showers 1982). Similarly, preservice student teachers could use a model of teaching when asked; however, more often than not the student teacher imitated the behavior of the cooperating teacher regardless of preservice training. Specifically, the young teachers-to-be tended to become less rewarding, more punishing, and less negotiating toward children. Also, they dominated the conversation more and asked fewer "higher order" questions. It took an extremely powerful training intervention to alter this general behavior pattern (Joyce, Brown & Peck, 1982). The powerful impact of the cooperating teacher has been well documented (Kilgore, 1979). Kilgore also found, however, that training cooperating teachers in the same models of teaching as the preservice students resulted in both cooperating teachers and student teachers utilizing the models more effectively and more frequently, and that pupil behavior and outcomes moved toward the intended outcomes of the model of teaching being used.

Summary and Discussion

I ndividual models of teaching generally have a strong research base. Many of the models were developed as a researcher's or theorist's answer to what effective teaching should be; other models were developed to enhance curricular programs. Early research on teaching models was generally comparative in nature, that is, one model or procedure was compared to another in an attempt to prove that one was better than the other. This was especially true concerning comparison of certain teaching models to the lecture method of teaching. Most researchers felt that what they espoused had to be more effective as a teaching process than the lecture. Each model (including the lecture) has subsequently been found to be effective, in some part, within a learning sequence. Teachers do teach in patterns or styles, and their teaching styles can be expanded with the addition of teaching models.

The concept of a teacher having a minimum "repertoire" of teaching models has been the focus of recent research. Teachers can learn and use a variety of teaching models if appropriate environmental and personality conditions are present. Students of teachers who use such a repertoire appear to gain in learning in the directions indicated by the models being used. Additionally, as teachers must teach to groups of students, and students have various learning styles, then it stands to reason that teachers should have a variety of teaching skills and models at their command in order to reach a greater number of students.

Finally, both preservice and inservice teachers can learn to operate a variety of teaching models and use them upon request or as needed. Experienced teachers can learn and implement a new model faster and with more understanding than an undergraduate in training. An appropriate number of models for a teaching repertoire has yet to be determined, but a teacher's preparation should include the ability to use at least one model from each family of models.

Instruction in models of teaching should become a major component of teacher education programs, especially at the methods course and field experience levels, with the research foundation being laid in the human development and learning course. Faculty should determine which models should be learned by preservice students in general methods as well as content specific methods courses. Special consideration should be given to those models that have a substantial research base such as those reviewed in this paper and to those presented by Bruning and Santmire, elsewhere in this document. Familiarity with models of teaching should help preservice students develop the type of needed decision-making skills presented by Walter elsewhere in this monograph.

Inclusion of models of teaching in the training program obligates the training institution to do two things to insure that the student has indeed learned and can apply the models. First, the training program must include a sequence that allows the student to learn the theory, see demonstrations, have practice and receive feedback (perhaps micro or peer teaching), and have opportunities to apply the model in the classroom during pre-student teaching and student teaching field experiences. The program must have a very strong intervention aspect in order to compensate for the fact that student teachers will imitate a cooperating teacher's behavior regardless of the training program. The second portion of the strategy would be to identify or train cooperating teachers in operation of the models of teaching being espoused by the training institution and then place the preservice students with those cooperating teachers.

References

Ausubel, D. (1963). *The psychology of meaningful verbal learning.* New York: Grune & Stratten, Inc.

Ausubel, D. (1968). *Educational psychology: A cognitive view.* New York: Holt, Rinehart & Winston.

Ausubel, D. (1978). In defense of advance organizers: A reply to the critics. *Review of Educational Research, 48(2).*

Barnes, B. R., & Clawson, E. V. (1975). Do advance organizers facilitate learning? *Review of Educational Research, 45(2).*

Becker, W. C., Engelmann, S., & Thomas, D. R. (1971). *Teaching: A course in applied psychology.* Chicago: Science Research Associates.

Becker, W. C., Engelmann, S., & Thomas, D. R. (1975a). *Teaching 1: Classroom management.* Chicago: Science Research Associates.

Becker, W. C., Engelmann, S., & Thomas, D. R. (1975b). *Teaching 2: Cognitive learning and instruction.* Chicago: Science Research Associates.

Brown, C. C. (1981). The relationship between teaching styles, personality and setting. In *Flexibility in teaching.* New York: Longman, Inc.

Bruner, J. S., Goodnow, J. J., & Austin, G. A. (1966). *A study of thinking.* New York: John Wiley & Sons, Inc.

Bruner, J. S., Goodnow, J. J., & Austin, G. A. (1977). *A study of thinking*. Huntington, NY: Robert E. Krieger.

Bruning, R. H. (1984). Key elements of effective teaching in the direct teaching model. (This volume.)

Eisner, E. (1983). The art and craft of teaching. *Educational Leadership, 40*, 4, Washington, DC: A.S.C.D.

Gage, N. L. (1979). *The scientific basis of the art of teaching*. New York: Teachers College Press, Columbia University.

Glasser, W. (1965). *Reality therapy*. New York: Harper & Row Publishers, Inc.

Harvey, O. J., Hunt, D. E., & Schroder, H. M. (1961). *Conceptual systems and personality organization*. New York: Wiley.

Hull, C. L. (1920). Quantitative aspects of the evolution of concepts. An experimental study. *Psychological Monographs, 28(2)*, Whole No. 124, 1-55.

Hunt, D. E. (1970). A conceptual level matching model for coordinating learner characteristics with educational approaches. *Interchange, 1(2)*.

Joyce, B. R., & Weil, M. L. (1972). *Models of teaching*. Englewood Cliffs, NJ: Prentice Hall, Inc.

Joyce, B. R. & Weil, M. L. (1980). *Models of teaching* (2nd ed.). Englewood Cliffs, NJ: Prentice Hall, Inc.

Joyce, B. R., Brown, C. C., & Peck, L. (1981). *Flexibility in teaching: An excursion into the nature of teaching and training*. New York: Longmon, Inc.

Joyce, B. R., & Showers, B. (1980, February). Improving inservice training: The messages of research. *Educational Leadership, 37*.

Joyce, B. R., & Showers, B. (1981). *Teacher training research: Working hypotheses for program design and directions for further study*. Paper presented at the annual meeting of the American Educational Research Association, Los Angeles, CA.

Joyce, B. R., & Showers, B. (1982, October). The coaching of teaching. *Educational Leadership, 40*.

Joyce, B. R., Wald, R., & Weil, M. L. (1981). Can teachers learn repertoires of models of teaching? In *Flexibility in teaching*. New York: Longman, Inc.

Kilgore, A. M. (1978). *Didactic teaching models: The oral presentation*. Unpublished manuscript, University of Nebraska, Lincoln, NE.

Kilgore, A. M. (1979, July-Aug). Pilot project shows definite link between pre-, in-service education. *Journal of Teacher Education*, Vol. XXX, No. 4.

Lawton, J. T., & Wanska, S. K. (1977). Advance organizers as a teaching strategy: A reply to Barnes and Clawson. *Review of Educational Research, 47(2)*.

Oliver, D., & Shaver, J. P. (1966). *Teaching public issues in the high school*. Boston: Houghton Mifflin Co.

Piaget, J. (1952). *The origins of intelligence in children*. New York: International University Press.

Rogers, C. (1971). *Client centered therapy*. Boston: Houghton Mifflin Co.

Rosenshine, B., & Furst, N. (1971). Research on teacher performance criteria. In B. O. Smith (Ed.), *Research in teacher education: A symposium.* Englewood Cliffs, NJ: Prentice Hall, Inc.

Santmire, T. E., & Friesen, P. H. (1984). A developmental analysis of research on effective teacher-student interactions: Implications for teacher preparation. (This volume.)

Schwab, J. J. (1965). Biological sciences curriculum study. *Biology teachers handbook.* New York: John Wiley & Sons, Inc.

Seperson, M. A., & Joyce, B. R. (1973, 1981). The relationship between the teaching styles of student teachers and those of cooperating teachers. In *Flexibility in teaching.* New York: Longman, Inc. (Reprinted from *Educational Leadership,* 1973).

Showers, B. (1983). *Transfer of training.* Paper presented at the annual meeting of the American Educational Research Association, Montreal, Canada.

Skinner, B. F. (1953). *Science and human behavior.* New York: Macmillan, Inc.

Stallings, J. (1983, November). *Implication for the research on teaching for teacher preparation.* A paper presented at the Nebraska Consortium for the Improvement of Teacher Education Workshop, Lincoln, Nebraska.

Stickel, W. E. (1972). *Effects of the Hilda Taba teaching strategies program on verbal behavior and attitudes of teachers.* Unpublished doctoral dissertation, United States International University, San Diego, CA.

Suchman, J. R. (1962). *The elementary school training program in scientific inquiry.* Report to the U.S. Office of Education, Project Title VII, Project 216. Urbana, IL: University of Illinois.

Taba, H. (1966). *Teaching strategies and cognitive functioning in elementary school children* (Cooperative Research Project 2404). San Francisco: San Francisco State College.

Thelan, H. (1960). *Education and the human quest.* New York: Harper and Row, Publishers, Inc.

Weil, M. L., & Murphy, J. (1982). Instructional Processes. In *Encyclopedia of educational research.* New York: The Free Press.

APPENDIX

MODELS OF TEACHING* ORGANIZED BY FAMILIES

Information Processing Models: A Selection

MODEL	MAJOR THEORIST	MISSION OR GOAL
Inductive Thinking Model	Hilda Taba	Designed primarily for development of inductive mental processes and academic reasoning or theory building, but these capacities are useful for personal and social goals as well.
Inquiry Training Model	Richard Suchman	
Scientific Inquiry	Joseph J. Schwab (also much of the Curriculum reform Movement of the 1960's)	Designed to teach the research system of a discipline, but also expected to have effects in other domains sociological methods may be taught in order to increase social understanding and social problem solving).
Concept Attainment	Jerome Bruner	Designed primarily to develop inductive reasoning, but also for concept development and analysis.
Cognitive Growth	Jean Piaget Irving Sigel Edmund Sullivan Lawrence Kohlberg	Designed to increase general intellectual development, especially logical reasoning, but can be applied to social and moral development as well (see Kohlberg, 1976).
Advance Organizer Model	David Ausubel	Designed to increase the efficiency of information-processing capacities to absorb and relate bodies of knowledge.
Memory	Harry Lorayne Jerry Lucas	Designed to increase capacity to memorize.

*From Models of Teaching by Bruce Joyce and Marsha Weil, 1980.

123

Personal Models: A Selection

MODEL	MAJOR THEORIST	MISSION OR GOAL
Nondirective Teaching	Carl Rogers	Emphasis on building the capacity for personal development in terms of self-awareness, understanding, autonomy, and self-concept.
Awareness Training	Fritz Perls William Schutz	Increasing one's capacity for self-exploration and self-awareness. Much emphasis on development of interpersonal awareness and understanding as well as body and sensory awareness.
Synectics	William Gordon	Personal development of creativity and creative problem solving.
Conceptual Systems	David Hunt	Designed to increase personal complexity and flexibility.
Classroom Meeting	William Glasser	Development of self-understanding and responsibility to oneself and one's social group.

Social Interaction Models: A Selection

MODEL	MAJOR THEORIST	MISSION OR GOAL
Group Investigation	Herbert Thelen John Dewey	Development of skills for participation democratic social process through combined emphasis on interpersonal (group) skills and academic inquiry skills. Aspects of personal development are important outgrowths of this model.
Social Inquiry	Byron Massialas Benjamin Cox	Social problem solving, primarily through academic inquiry and logical reasoning.
Laboratory Method	National Training Laboratory (NTL) Bethel, Maine	Development of interpersonal and group skills and, through this, personal awareness and flexibility.
Jurisprudential	Donald Oliver James Pl Shaver	Designed primarily to teach the jurisprudential frame of reference as a way of thinking about and resolving social issues.
Role Playing	Fannie Shaftel George Shaftel	Designed to induce students to inquire into personal and social values, with their own behavior and values becoming the source of their inquiry.
Social Simulation	Sarene Boocock Harold Guetzkow	Designed to help students experience various social processes and realities and to examine their own reactions to them, also to acquire concepts and decision-making skills.

Behavioral Models: A Selection

MODEL	MAJOR THEORIST	MISSION OR GOAL
Contingency Management	B. F. Skinner	Facts, concepts, skills.
Self-Control	B. F. Skinner	Social behavior/skills.
Relaxation	Rimm & Masters, Wolpe	Personal goals (reduction of stress, anxiety).
Stress Reduction	Rimm & Masters, Wolpe	Substitution of relaxation for anxiety in social situation.
Assertive Training	Wolpe, Lazarus, Salter	Direct, spontaneous expression of feelings in social situation.
Direct Training	Gagne Smith and Smith	Pattern of behavior, skills.

Implications from The Research on Teaching for Teacher Preparation

Jane A. Stallings

Vanderbilt University

Effective teaching was the focus of a great deal of research during the 1970s. This effort was reasonably rewarding. Many relationships between how teachers teach and what students learn were identified. The findings emerged from studies using a wide variety of methodologies. The question for this paper to consider is "What are the implications of those findings for teacher preparation?" In summarizing the papers prepared for the 1982 Conference on Research on Teaching held at Airlie House, Virginia, Gage (1982) says that findings from the research on teaching range along a continuum of strength.

> At the weakest extreme is what we might call a *shred*—a weak relationship based on a small sample or an ethnographer's glimmer of insight. Next is a *suggestion* that something mildly good will happen if teachers behave in a certain way. A *recommendation* follows from convincing evidence—a strong relationship or an educational connoisseur's ineluctable conviction. An *imperative* consists of a powerful recommendation—a moral cry for action. And finally, a *categorical imperative* is a moral law that is absolute and universally binding.

Needless to say, there are few findings in the latter category. Gage goes on to say, "Implications for practice need to be considered carefully. Large effect sizes do not necessarily have important implications. Small effect sizes may amount to more than shreds or suggestions. Perhaps, if we think about them wisely, they can support recommendations or even imperatives."

In order to know whether research findings are useful in the classroom, the findings must be translated into workable teacher training programs. Using research based curriculums, several training experiments have been conducted (Anderson, Evertson, & Brophy, 1979; Crawford et al., 1978; Good & Grouws, 1979; Stallings, Needels, & Stayrook, 1979). The training treatment teachers received in these experiments ranged from a detailed list of recommendations to a series of seven 2-1/2 hour training sessions with observation and feedback to guide and encourage continued teacher change. Notably, in all of the experiments, teachers changed their behavior and student achievement was significantly affected. The results of these several experiments are reported by Gage and Giaconia (1981).

Thus far, findings from the research on teaching have been used primarily to improve the instruction of inservice teachers. In the 1970s, comprehensive inservice training programs were financed by local, state, and national education agencies. An estimated $2000 per year per teacher was spent on inservice training during that period. This included the cost of programs such as Teacher Corps, Follow Through, Head Start, the staff development components of migrant education, bilingual education, special education, etc. Social changes required this massive effort to retrain teachers to help them work with mainstreamed handicapped students, multicultured student groups, recent immigrants, and low achieving students. The avenue for educational improvement was considered by educators and funding agents to be through the schools rather than through colleges preparing new teachers. The primary reason for this was that very few new teachers were being hired; fewer children were in schools and tenured teachers were staying in their jobs longer.

However, time passes, children grow up and produce more children, and tenured teachers grow older. According to the National Center for Educational Statistics, by 1985 we will need 689,000 new teachers, and 983,000 by 1990. This need will be created by the children of the baby boom children entering schools in the 1980s and the retirement of the many teachers who entered the work force in the 1950s to teach the baby boom children. The need to prepare new science and math teachers is particularly critical, for business and industry have been luring these teachers away from the schools.

The spotlight for educational improvement in the 1980s is on preservice education. The task of preparing a whole new cadre of teachers is a wonderfully challenging opportunity. Old and well worn curriculums must be examined in light of the knowledge and skills beginning teachers need to provide effective instruction in schools today. The 1982 Conference on Research on Teaching, upon which this paper is based, produced a synthesis of the most salient findings from schools and classrooms to that time.

As previously stated, the purpose of this paper is to consider the implications of the research on teaching to the curriculum and instruction of preservice education. Since teaching occurs within a school, the effective school findings are considered first in this paper. These are followed by the descriptive and statistical findings on classroom organization and management, instruction, and teacher expectations. A section on collaborative research describes a process rather than findings per se. Embedded in each section are suggestions of how these research findings might be incorporated into preservice programs. The final section considers some of the problems and challenges confronting those who are responsible for preparing new teachers.

The School Community

Schools have been defined as "loosely coupled systems in which the work of the teacher is largely independent of the principal's immediate supervision" (Purkey & Smith, 1982). While it may be generally true that teachers are sovereign in their own classrooms, they do operate within schools and are subject to policies and practices that may limit or enhance what happens in the classroom. For example, if policies regarding cuts and tardiness are clear and well enforced, students are in class more often; if there are few interruptions from the intercom or from students leaving the class for special activities, there is more time to provide instruction; if the discipline policy is clear, students behave better in class (Stallings & Mohlman, 1981; Glenn, 1981).

In academically effective schools, Purkey and Smith (1982) report a greater degree of (1) collaborative planning and collegial relationships, (2) sense of community (parents, teachers, and students), (3) clear goals and high expectations commonly shared, and (4) order and discipline. The leadership of the principal is a primary factor in effective schools.

Given these conditions, if a new teacher is lucky enough to be hired into an effective school, he/she may be expected to participate in decision making. Thus, some experience in collaborative planning and shared decision making would be helpful. This could be accomplished during teacher preparation through simulated staff meetings at which program decisions are made. Discussions with local school principals regarding how school policies are formed could acquaint the preservice teacher with school issues and a range of administrative leadership styles.

How school policies are made ranges from collaboration among teachers, parents, students, and administrators to top-down orders issued by the principals. The principal's leadership style may be supportive, guiding and collaborative, or very directive depending upon the situation. It would be helpful for preservice teachers to be aware of and thus prepared for a variety of leadership styles. Very clear rules for teachers, e.g., checking in, attending meetings, being on time, being available 30 minutes after school, can be helpful to a new teacher. The point is that preservice education should prepare teachers for several eventualities. (See Gates, Blanchard, & Hersey, 1976.)

In fact, leadership may not always come from the principal. Leadership sometimes comes from a few influential teachers with energy and vision (Berman & McLaughlin, 1976). Such teachers may initiate policy and/or control policy. The preservice teacher needs to be able to recognize these power groups and consider how to function through them.

Teacher unions or associations are other sources of power that affect the school community (Purkey & Smith, 1982). The preservice curriculum should include how unions or associations operate, how to influence them, and the options available. It would be informative to have a union or association representative discuss selected issues with preservice teachers.

Another influential sector of the school community is parents. Parent expectations and participation will differ by region, school size, grade level, and socioeconomic and ethnic background. It is of utmost importance that new teachers establish good rapport with parents and listen to their expectations. Without careful consideration, teachers may depend upon stereotypes of cultural groups and establish negative self-fulfilling prophecies for some groups of students (Hamilton, 1983).

Satisfied parents can be a great source of help and support (Purkey & Smith, 1982). Dissatisfied parents can hinder and hurt. The preservice curriculum should offer opportunities to observe a master teacher conducting parent conferences, meetings, and home visits. Parents can be helpful in increasing students' learning time. Duval County, Florida, has developed useful materials for parents to use with their children. The focus is toward helping children learn to learn at home. This county has been successful in raising student achievement through school and home cooperation. There is a unanimity of purpose and practice between home and school (Sang, 1982).

Attributes of Effective Classrooms

The preservice curriculum needs to be coordinated so that classrooms are considered total environments to be affected by teacher decisions. Physical things such as space, furniture, materials, curriculum, and time may be determined by others, but how they are used is determined by the teacher. The participants are also fixed, but the activities offered and the interactions that occur are determined by the teacher. Green and Smith (1982) make a convincing argument that teachers provide academic content and structure for student participation simultaneously; content and process are interactive. However, the total classroom environment is so complex that researchers have tended to study small pieces of that very large puzzle. The first piece in that puzzle to be considered here is space.

Space

Space and how it is used is important. In effective classrooms, Arlin (1979) reports that space is:

> divided into distinct areas furnished and equipped for specific activities. Equipment that must be stored can be removed and replaced easily, and each item has its own place. Traffic patterns facilitate movement around the room, and minimize crowding or bumping. Transitions between activities are accomplished efficiently following a brief signal or a few directions from the teacher, and the students seem to know where they are supposed to be, what they are supposed to be doing, and what equipment they will need.

Nash (1981) reports that preplanning of classroom space can maximize student use of materials and participation in activities. Preservice curriculum should provide the opportunity for potential teachers to arrange doll sized furniture in simulated classrooms of different sizes with 20 to 40 students. This would provide the experience of organizing a classroom and considering the issues Brophy mentions.

Use of Time

There is considerable research on the use of time in schools. Research in the 1970s indicates that more time is not necessarily better. A longer school day can simply mean longer lunch and recess periods (Harnischfeger & Wiley, 1978). Stallings' work in elementary and secondary schools did not indicate greater student achievement in longer school days or class periods. How the available time was used was the important factor (Stallings, 1975; Stallings, Needels, & Stayrook, 1979).

Fisher et al. (1978) report that on the average, children in California spent six hours in school a day. Of that time, only two to four hours were spent in instruction. Within that instructional time, students were engaged from 1.5 to 3.5. hours, and of the engaged time for the total school day, students were involved with appropriate materials only 36 minutes to 90 minutes. Preservice teachers should be made aware of these findings and consider how easy it is to waste those golden minutes.

Knowing that time should not be wasted does not provide much guidance for the beginning teacher. More specific information is needed regarding how effective teachers use their time. To this end Stallings and Mohlman (1981) assimilated four data sets from secondary schools and identified how effective teachers distributed their time across activities. They found that effective teachers spent 15 percent or less time in organizing or management tasks, 50 percent or more time in interactive instruction, and 35 percent or less time in monitoring seatwork (see Table 1). Effective teachers used some time to work with the total group, small groups, and individuals. While this distribution of time would not be appropriate for all grade levels or times of year, it is a framework that can help preservice teachers think about the use of available time.

Lesson Plans

Decisions about the use of time should be made through a careful daily, weekly, and long range plan. Shavelson (1983, p. 403) referring to Yinger's work (1977) reports the following pattern of teacher planning.

1. *Long range*—yearly planning for academic subjects.
2. *Term*—planning for academic subjects and certain materials.
3. *Monthly*—planning for basic academic units and necessary materials.
4. *Weekly*—planning for specific units and time allocation.
5. *Daily*—planning.

(Yinger, 1977, p. 172)

Specific skills are needed to prepare a daily and weekly plan. Madeline Hunter's widely used Instructional Skills Program offers a detailed five-step lesson plan. Many school districts and state departments of education are disseminating Hunter's strategies. Even though there is not solid evidence of the effectiveness of the program, a preservice curriculum should include exposure to the five-step lesson plan. A study is in progress to evaluate the relationship between teacher implementation of the Instructional Skills Program and student engaged rate and achievement (Stallings, Robbins, & Wolfe, 1983).

Long-range plans are also important. According to Joyce (1979), p. 75):

> Most of the important preactive decisions by teachers are long-term in their influence as opposed to the influence of lesson by lesson planning. Relatively early in the year, most teachers set up a series of conditions which were to be powerfully influential on the possibilities of decision making thereafter. Lesson planning, to the extent that it goes on consciously, involves the selection and handling of materials and activities within the framework that has been set up by the long-term decisions.

TABLE 1
TIME ALLOCATIONS

Organizing/Management Activities (15% or less)

(E) Take Roll	
(E) Make Announcements	
(E) Pass Materials	15%
(E) Make Expectations *Clear* for the Period:	Non Academic
Quality and Quantity of Work	
(S) Organize Groups	
(E) Clarify and Enforce Behavior Expectations	

Interactive Instructional Activities (50% or more)

(E) Review/Discuss Previous Work	
(E) Inform/Instruct New Concept Demonstrate/Give Examples Link to Prior Knowledge	
(E) Quesiton/Check for Understanding	85%
(S) Reteach Small Group (if necessary)	Academic
(S) Oral Drill and Practice	
(E) Summarize	

Teacher Monitoring/Guiding Seatwork (35% or less)
(I) Written Work
(I) Silent Reading

	KEY
E	*Total Class*
S	*Small Group*
L	*Large Group*
I	*Individual*

In spite of best laid plans, the lesson may not go that way. Research by linguists indicates that while a teacher may plan a lesson, the lesson itself is modified as the teacher and students interact with the materials and activities (Green & Smith, 1982). In summarizing several studies on planning, Shavelson (1982) suggests that prolific planning may be counter-productive if the teachers become single minded and do not adapt their lessons to student needs. Thus the preservice curriculum should incorporate strategies for planning lessons and develop an awareness for when and how to alter plans.

Classroom Organization and Management

There is no doubt that students in classrooms that are well managed perform better on achievement tests (Brophy, 1979; Fisher et al., 1980; Good, 1979; Rosenshine & Berliner, 1978). "Because successful classroom managers maximize the time their students spend engaged in academic activities, their students have more opportunities to learn and this shows up in superior performance on achievement tests" (Brophy, 1982). However, knowing this fact will not help the preservice teacher know how to do it. Observations by researchers Evertson, Anderson, and Emmer in both elementary and junior high schools (1980) were so specific that practice can be guided by them even for the first days of school. These researchers describe in detail how effective teachers established and carried out their management plans, and subsequently developed a set of checklists for teacher use. Preservice teachers should have the benefit of reviewing these materials.

Grouping is a part of classroom organization. Children are grouped within classrooms for several purposes. Traditionally, students were placed in ability groups (high, medium, and low) so that teachers could provide instruction that was appropriate to the approximate achievement levels of the children. This practice has raised serious controversy regarding children's self-images, motivation, and perceptions. Linguistic studies summarized by Green and Smith (1982) indicate that students in low groups have different input in terms of content, strategies for reading, and definitions of reading. Lessons for low groups consistently placed greater emphasis on pronunciation, grammar errors, and single word decoding. The high groups were encouraged to "go for the meaning;" their pronunciation and grammar errors were often ignored. Weinstein (1982) describes how children perceive the teachers' relationship to high and low achieving students. Students described as low achievers received more negative feedback and teacher direction, and more work and rule orientation than high achievers. High achievers were perceived as receiving higher expectations, more opportunity and choice than low achievers. No differences were documented in the perceived degree of supportive help. Unfortunately, we do not know the achievement effects upon the high and low achieving students who received differential treatment.

There is research from studies of reading and math that indicates ability grouping has a positive effect upon achievement. The Direct Instruction Follow Through Program (Becker, 1977) has consistently had a positive effect upon children within reading and math ability groups. This program does, however, allow for children to change from one group to another as their progress warrants. The National Follow Through Study also found a positive effect from ability grouping. Low achieving students profited in math from a longer period of study more than did high achieving students (Stallings, 1975).

When and how teachers work with each group is important. Work in progress indicates that it is more effective to work with the medium achievement reading group first, the low group second, and the high group last. In this manner, the lowest group, who are likely to have the shortest attention span, do not have as long a time at the beginning or end of the period to work independently (Stallings, 1983).

During group work, effective teachers make clear when students can ask questions and of whom they can ask questions. They do not allow students to interrupt during focused small group instruction (Evertson et al., 1981). However, Green and Smith (1982) report that this signaling of what is acceptable and what is not is a complex process. If teachers do not respond to students' requests for help as needed, the student has several alternatives: the student can (1) attempt to overcome the problem or make a decision on his/ her own, (2) ask another student for help, (3) switch to an alternative activity, or (4) approach the teacher anyway. Each decision carries a different outcome for the student. Instruction for preservice teachers should help make them aware of these student options and have strategies to assist students to stay on task until help can be offered.

Groupings are also used for cooperative learning and to establish good interpersonal relationships and group dynamics in the classroom. Several researchers have developed methods to bring about student cooperation (Aronson et al., 1978; Slavin, 1980). They have developed a variety of activities in which students of different achievement levels form groups that have a task to complete requiring the participation of all students. In one approach, each member of the group possesses at least one key item of unique information which is essential to the group's success. The problem encountered encourages everyone to participate. In some cooperative approaches, participants receive a group score rather than an individual score. The group score could be based upon the gain made by each participant. Such procedures motivate the high, medium, and low achieving students to cooperate and achieve.

It is important to note that children are not likely to know how to work in groups productively unless some training is provided. Wilcox (1972) found that students trained to lead groups by encouraging all to participate and being certain that everyone had a turn were better at solving specific problems than were untrained or leaderless groups. The trained student leader groups were also better group problem solvers than were classroom teachers, who tended to do all the problem solving themselves. It is important that preservice teachers be exposed to the cooperative group learning research since it offers an alternative to competitive and rote learning.

Disruptive Student Behavior

The findings on disruptive behavior are very clear in all of our studies. In classrooms where students evidence more misbehavior, less time is spent on task and less achievement gain is made by students. There are many techniques effective teachers use to manage student behavior. The first days of school study by Evertson, Anderson, and Emmer (1980) yielded some specific recommendations: define rules and penalties before school starts (co-ordinate with school rules), teach rules and procedures to students during the first days of school, consistently monitor and reinforce rules, reward acceptable behavior and punish misbehavior.

There are some behavior management programs such as the Assertive Discipline Training Program (Cantor) and the Classroom Management Training Program (Jones) which bring peer pressure to bear upon individuals. These programs offer rewards for good behavior (special games, activities, script, recognition) and withdraw privileges for bad behavior. These programs are effective in stopping the behavior, but they do not necessarily solve the problem.

Problems of an interpersonal nature need to be solved. Glasser's *Schools Without Failure* (1969) offers group problem solving methods and techniques to help students develop responsibility for their own behavior. Brophy (1982) summarizes the ten steps of this process (p. 35-36). While there is little systematic research on the Glasser program, survey data (1977) indicate fewer referrals to the office, fighting, or suspensions among students in classes implementing this program.

The preservice curriculum should include several approaches to controlling disruptive behavior. Of the several hundred teachers with whom I have worked and the student teachers interviewed in the last several months, there is solid agreement that most lacking in their preparation for teaching were techniques for managing classroom behavior.

Instruction

Now that the stage is set—furniture and materials placed, lessons planned, and strategies ready for dealing with disruptive behavior—instruction is about to begin. Instruction can and should follow several formats determined by the participants, subject matter, and objectives of the lesson. There are no panaceas.

Three aspects of learning have yielded useful implications for classroom teaching: these are (1) memory, (2) understanding, and (3) reasoning or problem solving. All three of these functions are necessary for students to process and use information.

Memory. Memory skills are essential for lower elementary students to succeed in basic reading, writing, and computation. Ample research in the 1970s indicates that a very structured, carefully sequenced approach is effective in developing memory skills/basic skills. Rosenshine (1982) in summarizing this literature says:

> In general, to the extent that students are younger, slower, and/or have little prior background, teachers are most effective when they:

● structure the learning experience

● proceed in small steps but at a rapid pace

● give detailed and more redundant instructions and explanations

- have a high frequency of questions and overt, active practice
- provide feedback and corrections, particularly in the initial stages of learning new material
- have a success rate of 80% or higher in initial learning
- divide seatwork assignments into smaller segments or devise ways to provide frequent monitoring
- provide for continued student practice (overlearning) so that they have a success rate of 90-100%

The interactions are started by the teacher presenting a small bit of information, asking a question, and calling for an individual or group response. Praise is offered if the answer is correct and correction is given if the response is incorrect (Anderson, Evertson, & Brophy, 1979).

Research of the past few years shows that most students can, through sufficient drill and practice, memorize most facts that are important for them to have available through immediate recall. The curriculum for preservice teachers should include instructional practice in using quick paced interactions when children need to memorize material.

Understanding. In addition to facilitating students' memorization of facts, instruction should also develop students' understanding of the lesson content. Cognitive psychologists have studied linkages between new information and prior knowledge. Teachers need to help students make these linkages. Every student walks into the classroom with some experiences and knowledge, but this experience differs widely, especially among children from varied socio-economic and ethnic backgrounds. This is one reason why it is important for teachers to understand the children's culture. How the teacher structures the new information makes a difference in what students will be able to link to their existing information. Calfee (1981) describes the mind as a filing system where there are hooks or pegs on which to hang information. This filing system is essentially the long-term memory from which the information can be retrieved and used in other situations.

For information to be filed, it must first be noticed. Broadbent (1975) wrote that only some of the information presented will receive attention, and if this selection is not decided deliberately, it will certainly be decided by chance factors. If something is not noticed at the time it happens, it has hardly any chance of affecting long term memory (or the filing system as Calfee describes it). It is the teacher's role to be certain that students have noticed the information and made a link with existing information, thus guaranteeing storage in long-term memory.

The importance of teachers' checking for understanding was shown in a study conducted by Webb (1980). In a group problem solving task, those students who received an explanation after making an error solved the problem correctly on another trial. The explanation did not have to be directed toward the student, but could have been directed toward another student within the same group. Those students who never received explanations after an error were not able to solve the problem on the second trial.

Some educational programs, such as Madeline Hunter's Instructional Skills, include a step that requires teachers to check for student understanding before proceeding with instruction. If students do not understand, the teacher restructures the task and provides different examples and experiences to build the required background knowledge. The effects of this model are being tested (Stallings, Robbins, & Wolfe, 1983).

While the theory on student understanding and the need for linkage is strong, the research findings are meager to date. The studies tend to have small samples, and experiments that teach teachers to use strategies that will increase understanding and lead to testable student outcomes are generally lacking. More studies such as Webb's are needed. Nevertheless, it is important to include this research in the preservice curriculum even if it is still a twinkle in the researcher's eye.

Problem Solving/Reasoning. The need to train students in problem-solving or reasoning skills has been receiving increasing attention, both from the educational system and from industry. In a recent survey of electronics firms in California's Silicon Valley, business leaders were asked to identify the skills most lacking in their recently hired employees, and which skills the educational system should help students to develop to become effective employees. The majority of the respondents reported that the schools should help students develop problem solving skills, for such skills were needed by employees at all levels (Needels, 1982). The respondents reported that at the present, many of their recently hired employees, whether high school or college graduates, were deficient in that cognitive area.

G. H. Hanford, President of the College Board, notes that, "The decade-long decline in test scores appears largely due to the fact that reasoning ability in secondary schools is not what it used to be. In recent years, students in lower grades show marked improvement in reading, writing, and other basic skills, but students fall behind when problems get more complex." The College Board is currently funding a study to identify ways reasoning and problem solving can be taught (1983).

One of the difficulties in studying problem solving has been the lack of group administered tests that can examine the thinking skills of young children. The tests usually require individual administration and this prohibits large scale studies. Another problem is in identifying and measuring the classroom teaching skills expected to be related to gain in thinking skills. One anomaly is a study of 52 Follow Through classrooms (Stallings, 1975) which reports the relationship between scores on a group administered test of non-verbal problem solving skills and teaching behaviors. These findings indicate that student scores were higher on that test in classrooms where the structure allowed students to take more initiative. In such classrooms, students asked more questions, worked more independently with manipulative materials, and worked more often on group tasks in cooperative activities. Teachers asked more thought-provoking questions and provided less overt praise and correction. The lessons were not quick paced such as those used to develop memory skills.

Inquiry methods are expected to develop problem solving skills. Collins and Stevens (1982) identified instructional strategies used by expert teachers who use inquiry methods effectively. The authors identified five strategies: (1) systematic variation of examples, (2) counter examples, (3) entrapment strategies, (4) hypothesis identification strategies, and (5) hypothesis evaluation strategies. Even though the teachers observed by Collins and Stevens taught different content areas, the authors reported that these strategies were consistently used by all the teachers, thus the strategies most likely are not domain specific but can be applied to different content domains.

Preservice teachers need to be trained to think of the psychological processes and structures which the student must develop to produce the desired behavioral objectives. Any one lesson could require drill and practice, checks for understanding, and problem solving. It is the instructional repertoire that teachers need, and the knowledge of which strategy is likely to develop memory, understanding, or reasoning. The important thing is that preservice teachers do not embrace extreme or singular points of view. Broadbent (1975), in speaking of extremes, says that:

> life certain strategies of encoding the outside world, of organizing memory, and of proceeding from one step in an operation to the next, and that these may be highly general in their later use. The successful teacher, of course, has always known this, but in standing out for the middle ground between mechanical drill on the one hand and the abandonment of all positive teaching on the other, he/she can now claim the support of contemporary cognitive psychology (p. 175).

Teacher Judgment and Expectations

All teachers make judgments about students' abilities and develop a set expectations which guide the curriculums they offer and the instructional strategies they use. Teacher judgments of student achievement are based upon student reputations and observations of classroom behavior, work habits, products, classroom participation, and test scores. Although these judgments are fairly accurate, they tend to impact upon expectations for low achieving students in a self-fulfilling way.

In a summary of studies on teacher expectations, Brophy and Good (1974) indicate that students for whom teachers held low expectations were treated less well than other students. They tended to be seated farther away from the teacher. They received less eye contact and were smiled at less often. They received less instruction, had fewer opportunities to learn new materials, and were asked to do less work. Teachers called on these students less often and tended to ask them simple rote answer questions. They were given less time to respond and fewer guides or probing questions when their answers were wrong. They remained low achieving students.

In an effort to change teacher and student perceptions of low achieving students, Morine-Dershimer (1983) trained a group of teachers to ask higher level questions of low achieving students. The questions elicited ideas, hunches, opinions. When students in the class were asked to check the names on a list of these who made good contributions to the class discussion, low achieving students' names were checked. In classrooms where teachers asked low achieving students simple questions, these students were not rated as making contributions. This point is important. If teachers do not expect that students can take part in a higher level discussion, these students are not even given a chance. In the case of high achieving students, high achievement is reinforced, and similarly, low achieving students' low achievement is reinforced.

When asked to list the outstanding qualities of the best teacher they ever had, a national sample of school administrators, teachers, and parents most often mentioned high expectations. Audience responses included, "He challenged me." She made me think I could do it." "He thought I could, so I did." She always made me stretch a little bit higher." "He never let me off the hook.

Based upon clinical and mildly good empirical evidence, there are implications that teacher judgments and expectations do impact upon student learning in terms of what is offered to students and how students perceive each other. According to Gage's continuum of importance (1982), it seems "imperative" that the teacher preparation curriculum include exposure to the teacher judgment and expectation literature.

Collaborative Research

In order to continue to learn about effective instruction, the preservice teacher needs the opportunity to develop research skills. The teacher preparation courses should provide opportunities for students to develop questions which can be examined through naturalistic recordings, structured observations, criterion tests, surveys, or interviews.

The importance of research skills is exemplified by a project in San Diego conducted by Tikunoff, Ward, and Griffin (1979). The framework of this project required teachers at one school to select one pressing problem to study in depth. After several brainstorming sessions, the teachers decided to study classroom interruptions. With the assistance of the researchers, they developed methods to record the nature, purpose, and length of interruptions. The researchers helped the teachers process these data and write the results in a manner that could guide school practice. The beauty of this project is that teachers selected their most pressing problems and developed solutions.

During the project, the teachers were guided to read some of the research on teaching literature. Although classroom teachers expected it to be formidable, with a little help they did interpret and discuss the implications of the findings. Most classroom teachers do not have this opportunity and research studies remain formidable. It is the responsibility of preservice education to expose students to research terminology and possible flaws in re-

139

search designs. They may be pressed to conduct their own studies on the issues that matter to them.

Implications, Problems, and Solutions

Many recommendations have been made for inclusion of research findings in the teacher preparation curriculum. At this point, teacher educators may be considering all of the constraints placed by state legislatures or firmly entrenched programs. While state required course titles may be problematic, might it be possible to change the content and focus of the course while keeping the name? Most likely the process for teaching the courses could be changed without upsetting the system. It is this author's contention that the process of teaching teachers must become much more participatory.

In the freshman year, why not require education students to learn to use a simple well-focused observation instrument. For example, have them record in a real school classroom who the teacher speaks to and the nature of the interaction. (See the Attachment for simple seating chart observations.) Next, have the student discuss what they saw and contrast that with findings from research. There are some clearly written pieces free from jargon. (Anderson, Evertson, & Brophy, 1979, is one.) Each year, students should learn to use more complex observation systems and make naturalistic recordings. Let student teachers do peer observations and give each other feedback.

Incorporate the research on teaching into the methods courses and foundation classes. Within this structure students should be continually challenged to develop good questions about teaching and learning, to generate solutions, and to test ideas.

Another means to increase participation is to have the preservice teacher interact with school principals and teachers as they learn about the school community. Have a variety of excellent teachers and principals lead discussions and answer the preservice students' questions on a regular basis. The variety is important because there isn't a best style or solution to every situation. Good teaching is the matter of finding the right key to unlock knowledge for each student. A good locksmith has an assortment of keys and the expertise to know which key might fit. And so it is with teaching; a teacher needs a pocket full of keys and knowledge enough to make reasonable judgments about what will fit. The fortitude to keep trying is also necessary. While there is a knowledge base of good instruction, the teacher must also be a good learner. In this age of rapidly developing technology, even the graduates of 1983 will be left behind if they do not have learning skills and know how to use information.

References

Anderson, L., Evertson, C., & Brophy, J. (1979). An experimental study of effective teaching in first grade reading groups. *Elementary School Journal, 79,* 193-223.

Arlin, M. (1979). Teacher transitions can disrupt time flow in classrooms. *American Educational Research Journal, 16,* 42-56.

Aronson, E. (1978). *The jigsaw classroom.* Beverly Hills, CA: Sage.

Becker, W. C. (1977). Teaching reading and language to the disadvantaged— what we have learned from field research. *Harvard Educational Review, 47,* 518-543.

Berman, P., & McLaughlin, M. (1976). Implementation of educational innovation. *Educational Forum,* XL (3), 347-370.

Broadbent, D. (1975). Cognitive psychology and education. *British Journal of Educational Psychology, 45,* 162-176.

Brophy, J., & Good, T. (1974). *Teacher-student relationships: Causes and consequence.* New York: Holt, Rinehart & Winston.

Brophy, J. (1979). *Teacher praise: A functional analysis.* Paper presented to American Psychological Association.

Brophy, J. (1982). *Classroom organization and management.* Paper presented to the Conference on Research on Teaching, Airlie House, Virginia.

Calfee, R., & Shefelbine, J. (1981). A structured model of teaching. In Lewey and DeNevo (Eds.), *Evaluation roles in education.* New York: Cordon and Breck.

Collins, A., & Stevens, A. (1982). Goals and strategies of inquiry teachers. In R. Glaser (Ed.), *Advances in instructional psychology, Vol. II.* Hillsdale, NJ: Lawrence Erlbaum Associates.

Crawford, J., Gage, N. L., Corno, L., Stayrook, N., Mitman, A., Schunk, D., & Stallings, J. (1978). An experiment on teacher effectiveness and parent-assisted instruction in the third grade, (Vol. I-III). Center for Educational Research, Stanford, CA.

Evertson, C., Anderson, L., & Emmer, E. (1980). Effective management at the beginning of the school year. *Elementary School Journal, 80,* 219-231.

Evertson, C., Anderson, L., & Emmer, E. (1980). Effective management at the beginning of the school year in junior high classes. University of Texas at Austin: Research and Development Center for Teacher Education.

Evertson, C., Emmer, E., Clements, B., Sanford, J., Worsham, M., & Williams, E. (1981). Organizing and managing the elementary school classroom. University of Texas at Austin: Research and Development Center for Teacher Education.

Fisher, C. W., Filby, N. N., Marliave, R. S., Cahern, L. S., Dishaw, M. M., Moore, J. E., & Berliner, D. (1978). *Teaching behaviors, academic learning time and student achievement: Final report of Phase III-B, Beginning Teacher Evaluation Study.* Far West Regional Laboratory, San Francisco, CA.

Fisher, C., Berliner, D., Filby, N., Marliave, R., Cahen, L., & Dishaw, M. (1980). Teaching behaviors, academic learning time, and student achievement: An overview. In C. Denham & A. Lieberman (Eds.), *Time to learn.* Washington, DC: National Institute of Education.

Gage, N., & Giaconia, R. (1981). Teaching practices and student achievement: Causal connections. *New York University Education Quarterly, 13*(3), 2-9.

Gage, N. (1982). *When does research on teaching yield implications for practice?* Palo Alto, CA: Stanford University.

Gates, P., Blanchard, K., & Hersey, P. (1976, February). Diagnosing education leadership problems: A situational approach. *Educational Leadership*, 348-354.

Glasser, W. (1977). Ten steps to good discipline. *Today's Education, 66*, 61-63.

Glasser, W. (1969). *Schools without failure.* New York: Harper and Row.

Good, T. (1979). Teacher effectiveness in the elementary school: What we know about it now. *Journal of Teacher Education, 6*, 105-113.

Good, T. L. & Grouws, D. A. (1979). The Missouri mathematics effectiveness project: An experimental study in fourth-grade classrooms. *Journal of Educational Psychology, 71*, 335-362.

Green, J., & Smith, D. (1982). *Teaching and learning: A linguistic perspective.* A paper presented to the Conference on Research on Teaching, Airlie House, Virginia.

Hamilton, S. F. (1983). The social side of schooling: Ecological studies of classrooms and schools. *The Elementary School Journal, 83*(4), 313-334.

Hanford, G. (1983, January 29). As quoted in the *San Francisco Chronicle*, p. 3.

Harnischfeger, A., & Wiley, D. (1978, March). *Conceptual and policy issues in elementary school teacher learning.* Paper presented at the annual meeting of the American Educational Research Association, Toronto, Canada.

Joyce, B. (1978-79). Toward a theory of information processing in teaching. *Education Research Quarterly, 3*, 66-67.

Morine-Dershimer, G. (1983). Instructional strategy and the "creation" of classroom status. *American Educational Research Journal, 20*(4), 645-661.

Nash, B. (1981). The effects of classroom spatial organization on four- and five-year-old children's learning. *British Journal of Educational Psychology, 51*, 144-155.

Needels, M. (1982). Industry's willingness to collaborate with the education system: A survey of California's Silicon Valley. Menlo Park, CA: SRI International.

Purkey, S., & Smith, M. (1982, February). *Effective schools--A review.* A paper presented to the Conference on Research on Teaching, Airlie House, Warrenton, Virginia.

Rosenshine, B. & Berliner, D. (1978). Academic engaged time. *British Journal of Teacher Education, 4*, 3-16.

Rosenshine, B. (1982). *Teaching functions in instructional programs.* Paper presented to the Conference on Research on Teaching, Airlie House, Virginia.

Rutter, M., Maughan, B., Mortimore, P., & Ouston, J. (1979). *Fifteen thousand hours.* Cambridge, MA: Harvard University Press.

Sang, H. (1982, October). Education—A family affair. Jacksonville, Florida: *The Newsletter.*

Schlechty, P., & Vance, V. (1982, February). *Recruitment, selection and retention: The shape of the teaching force.* Paper presented to the Conference on Research on Teaching, Airlie House, Warrenton, Virginia.

Shavelson, R. J. (1983). Review of research on teachers' pedagogical judgments, plans, and decisions. *The Elementary School Journal, 83*(4), 392-413.

Shavelson, R. J. (1982). Review of research on teachers' pedagogical judgments, plans and decisions. Los Angeles, CA: The Rand Corporation and The University of California.

Slavin, R. (1980). Cooperative learning. *Review of Educational Research, 50,* 315-342.

Stallings, J. (1975, December). Implementations and child effects of teaching practices in Follow Through classrooms. *Monographs of the Society for Research in Child Development, 40,* 7-8.

Stallings, J., Needels, M., & Stayrook, N. (1979). *How to change the process of teaching basic reading skills in secondary schools.* Final report to the National Institute of Education. SRI, International, Menlo Park, CA.

Stallings, J. & Mohlman, G. (1981). *School policy, leadership style, teacher change and student behavior in eight schools.* Final Report prepared for the National Institute of Education, Washington, DC.

Stallings, J., Robbins, P., & Wolfe, P. (1983). A staff development program to increase student learning time and achievement. Napa, CA.

Tikunoff, W., Ward, B., & Griffin, G. (1979). *Interactive research and development on teaching, final report.* San Francisco, CA: Far West Laboratory for Educational Research and Development.

Webb, N. (1980). A process outcome analysis of learning in group and individual settings. *Journal of Educational Psychology, 15,* 69-83.

Weinstein, R. (1982). *Student perceptions of schooling.* Paper presented to the Conference on Research on Teaching, Airlie House, Virginia.

Wilcox, M. (1972). *Comparison of elementary school children's interactions in teacher-led small groups.* Unpublished doctoral dissertation, Stanford University, CA.

Yinger, R. (1977). *A study of teacher planning: Description and theory development using ethnographic and information processing models.* Unpublished doctoral dissertation, Michigan State University.

Reference Notes

Cantor, Lee. *Assertive Discipline* training program. Lee Cantor and Associates, 1553 Euclid Street, Santa Monica, California 90404.

Hunter, Madeline. *Increasing Teacher Effectiveness* training program. UCLA, Los Angeles, California.

Jones, Fredric H. *Classroom Management Training Program.* 64 Alta Vista Drive, Santa Cruz, California 95060.

ATTACHMENT

TEACHER'S INTERACTIONS WITH STUDENTS
SEATING CHART

This data is to be collected throughout the selected class period.

A simple way to collect information on the teacher's interaction patterns is to record on a seating chart each time the teacher speaks to an individual student. The coding can be as follows:

? = Teacher asks a student a direct question: "Johnny, what is the spelling of the word 'voyage'?

(?) = Teacher asks student an open-ended, thought-provoking question: "Ursula, what do you think will happen next in this story?"

1 = Teacher checks for understanding: "Tell us in your words, Maria, what photo-synthesis means."

    = Teacher makes a comment or response: "Flora, your hair looks nice today."

+ = Teacher praises or supports a response: "Very good, Jose, 'forty-two' is the correct answer."

C = Teacher corrects a students response: "No, Barbara, that is wrong."; or "The correct answer should have been 'Mark Twain'."

G = Teacher corrects *and guides* a response: "Janice, try spelling the word one letter at a time, according to how it sounds, and see if you can figure it out."

− = Teacher reprimands behavior: "Martin, be quiet!"

On the next page, we see an example where the teacher has asked Sue a direct question, praised, asked another question, guided, and praised.

These data can help teachers see to whom they are speaking and the nature of the interaction. It will also provide a frequence count of the questions asked, praise given, reprimands, and so forth.

NOTE: If the classroom seating takes a different form than the seating chart; for example, tables are arranged in a horseshoe formation instead of rows of desks; then the seating chart should be redrawn to conform to the actual classroom arrangement. The important thing is to get each student's name in the right place on the seating chart.

TEACHER'S INTERACTIONS WITH STUDENTS
SEATING CHART
DATE: _____ SCHOOL: _____

Mrs. Smith			

Flora ?G+	Mark / /	Betty	Joe (?)+

Jose	Susan ?+,?G+	Robert ?C	Donna

Ursula —	Daniel	Ellen	Bill —

Sharon —	Jack	Lee —	Mary

Instructions:

1. Fill in student's names in appropriate seats. Fill in the date.
2. Each time the teacher speaks to an individual student, record the appropriate code in the student's box.

Codes: ? = Asks a direct question
(?) = Asks an open-ended question
1 = Makes a comment or response

+ = Praises or supports a response
C = Corrects a response
G = Corrects and guides a response
− = Reprimands behavior

Stallings Teaching and Learning Institute

The American Federation of Teaachers Educational Research And Dissemination Program

Lovely H. Billups

American Federation of Teachers

Historically, there has existed a gap between educational research and classroom practice. The exchange of research information has largely been limited to researchers among themselves and/ or with college and university professors. In its original form, research is rarely of length, form or language that can be used by most classroom teachers. Moreover, the sometimes contradictory nature of research results causes skepticism by potential teacher-users who are often confused about which "authority source" to accept.

Traditional methods of disseminating research to teachers have been largely unsuccessful. Much research information gets as far as a state education agency or a district central office and then "reappears" as mandated programs for teacher implementation under the supervision of central office people and school administrators. Teachers who are expected to carry out the program usually have been excluded from the developmental process. The result has been that the direct implementers of the instructional process with students remain aloof from the educational research base. Often, this contributes to poor practical application of research concepts.

Philosophically, the leadership of the American Federation of Teachers (AFT) has long been inclined to believe that teaching is more than an art. It is also a science for which skills can be acquired by those who perform as teachers. Convinced that the results of educational research generated over the past two decades could be of practical value to teachers, AFT decided that the union, as an organization of professional peers, could develop a dissemination mechanism designed to bridge the gap between research and practice. NIE funded an AFT proposal to pilot this process and a two-year program was launched in January 1981.

Based on interactions with teachers through the Educational Issues Department, AFT realized that teachers held as a priority among their concerns a desire for help in better managing the classroom environment in which the teaching/learning process takes place. Disruptive student behavior, they re-

146

ported, was inhibiting their effectiveness as teachers; hence, AFT decided to focus on research findings related to classroom management and effective teaching. In distinguishing between the two areas, which are interdependent, we decided to identify classroom management studies as being those related to the behavioral or managerial aspect of teaching and teaching effectiveness studies as those related to the instructional process (Weber, 1980).

The AFT project was a unique undertaking. First, the union broke stereotypical bonds by taking a strong leadership role in the professional aspect of teachers' lives by collaborating with researchers, thus bridging a tremendous gap. Second, NIE funds were used for direct dissemination of research information to teachers. Third, teachers participated in an educational program on the basis of their individual worth as experienced practitioners without the threat of administrative judgments, negative evaluations or district mandates.

The two-year NIE funding period provided for program development and implementation in three urban pilot sites: New York City, San Francisco and Washington, D.C. As part of the process, a report documenting project outcomes was produced by the three project staff members who were hired to design the program and provide technical assistance to the project sites. The project staff consisted of two veteran classroom teachers who also had experience as teacher trainers and program developers. Much of their time was spent in the field carrying out local site development and training. Another member of the staff had experience in research usage and functioned as a technical assistant whose primary responsibilities were research identification and translation. The Director of the project was also Director of AFT's Educational Issues Department. All three staff members contributed to the writing of research training materials which resulted in the production of an *AFT Educational Research and Dissemination Training and Resource Manual.*

Identifying the Research

Project staff, with assistance from a three-member Advisory Board (Ann Lieberman, Teachers College, Columbia University; Lee Shulman, Institute for Research on Teaching at Michigan State University and presently at Stanford University; and Beatrice Ward, Deputy Director of Far West Educational Laboratory) identified usable research by establishing and then applying certain criteria. One of the major criteria was that the research addressed needs as perceived by teachers; a second criterion was that the research concepts were conducive to practical application in the classroom. Research findings which *could not* be replicated by classroom teachers either individually or collectively were not seen as usable in this teacher-oriented program. Additionally, the research selected had to be generic in scope, having implications for use across all grade levels and disciplines, since the teachers with whom we worked were teaching classes from pre-school to high school. Moreover, the findings from the research had to be fairly consistent in that they stemmed from a "validated" body of knowledge which consistently signalled a clear message about effective teaching practices. Finally, we used studies that were *translatable*, meaning that the statistical data was already interpreted. In some cases, original studies and/or specific researchers were consulted for clarification. Research studies by Anderson, Berliner, Brophy, Doyle, Emmet, Evertson, Fisher, Kounin, Gage, McDonald, Rosenshine, Soar and Stallings were among those suggested by the program's Advisory Board. Based on our experiences with these researchers, we were able to broaden our network of resources.

Selecting Teachers
To Work in the Program

Adhering to research findings on effective dissemination practices which advised that loyalty to the governing organization is an important factor in promoting effective participation, we identified loyalty and commitment to the union as one criterion for selecting program participants. We decided to designate these persons as TRLs (Teacher Research Linkers). In addition to union loyalty, we sought out teachers who were perceived as "good teachers" by their peers, were willing to learn, willing to try new ideas, and who were *trusted* and *respected* by their peers. Later we discovered that it was important for TRLs to be willing to commit ample time to the program, to be willing to express ideas and opinions, and to be able to share what they learned with other teachers. Each of the pilot sites used a process unique to its local needs in identifying these teachers as well as the person who would serve as Local Site Coordinator of the program. Aside from the three Local Site Coordinators, fifty-three teachers served as TRLs in the pilot program; the largest number of participants were at the New York site and the smallest group was in San Francisco.

Involvement of the TRLs

Teacher Research Linkers met with AFT program staff on an average of once every three-and-one-half weeks. Research training sessions were devoted to discussion and review of the "translated" research studies, which were always mailed to the participants well in advance of the session. We decided that it was more advantageous to the adult learner (Kidd, 1973) to have previous contact with the materials so that discussions could be held on a peer-equity level than to have a pedagogical expert-lecture-learner approach.

It was important that we attempt to neutralize teachers' negative attitudes about the value of educational research. Most of the TRLs were, at point of entry into the project, as leary as other teachers on classroom application of research concepts. We consistently reinforced the nonthreatening, nonjudgmental aspects of the process and demonstrated that we valued teachers as individuals, recognizing their personalized teaching styles as being very important to the ways in which they would assimilate the research information into their practice.

We found that teachers enjoyed making contributions to the discussions based on their classroom experiences and that they tended to question or propose changes, based on their teaching experiences. We emphasized that we valued their input as practicing teachers and that often the research findings would not be "brand new" to them but would serve to validate effective practice. Sometimes we used a portion of the training sessions to work through training activities which were developed as classroom-oriented experiences to make the research concepts more realistic to teachers. These activities involved role-playing situations, classroom simulations, and case studies, and were for the most part designed by the two experienced teachers on the AFT program staff.

Between sessions, TRLs were required to implement some of the teaching strategies suggested by the research in their own classrooms. Decisions on what to implement were made by each TRL, based on documentation of research-based strategies that were currently incorporated into their teaching practice and those which they felt they would like to try. Feedback on the results of these efforts was delivered to the group at the next session. This proved to be vital information in terms of "personalizing" the application of the research at grade, school or district levels. TRLs would report "This does not appear to be effective with middle-school-aged children," or "I found that my second graders reacted very positively to this change." Feedback was also forthcoming from other teachers in the schools. TRLs reported that as other teachers noticed changes they had made, e.g., room arrangement, they would inquire as to why the change had been made and how it was working.

Dissemination

M any TRLs began their duties as disseminators at the one-to-one level. This supported our concept of concentrating on building-level dissemination to reduce teacher isolation and to provide continuous on-the-spot support to teachers who used the research techniques. For years, our membership had complained that often they are inserviced by outside experts who are inaccessible to teachers once they have completed their presentations. Teachers say that they have often abandoned innovative practices because of a lack of these back-up services. Therefore, our TRLs were encouraged to share at the building level and to participate in large group sessions primarily as a means to encourage more in-depth involvement with the research, rather than one-shot workshop presentations.

Some of the TRLs, especially those from New York City, were experienced teacher trainers (Teacher Center-Teacher Specialists). Where the TRLs were experienced, dissemination of the information started almost as soon as the TRL was comfortable with his grasp of the material. At the other sites, we had to develop the TRLs as "experts" on the research knowledge and also help them to develop skills as disseminators. This involved a four-step cycle: training, planning, practice, and presentation. We shared information on Adult Learning Theory to help TRLs work with other teachers and we held in-group practice sessions during which TRLs developed effective ways to present the research information.

Eventually, 53 TRLs across the three sites, in addition to members of the AFT program staff, had reached most of the staff in the 40 schools where TRLs were located, in addition to another 2,500 teachers who attended system-wide workshops at local sites, local and national AFT QuEST (Quality Educational Standards in Teaching) conferences, and national union and education organization conferences.

Reactions to the Research

Studies used during the program period included:

Beginning of the Year Classroom Management (Emmer, Evertson, & Anderson, 1980)

Teacher Praise (Brophy, 1981)

Direct Instruction (Rosenshine, 1980; Good and Grouws, 1979; Stallings, 1980)

Group Management (Kounin, 1970)

Time on Task (Fisher, 1980)

Although the AFT Educational Research and Dissemination program did not scientifically document change in teacher practice, we have substantial testimonial data to support the belief that TRLs made real changes in practice as a direct result of their involvement in the program. We are convinced of the validity of this input from teachers because of the voluntary, nonthreatening, nonjudgmental aspects of the program. Teachers had nothing to gain from falsifying reports. Feedback came in the form of self-reports (Research Action and Reaction Forms) which were recorded by the TRLs during the two years they participated in the program. These documents required teachers to note the research-based strategies that were currently built into their teaching behaviors and then describe the strategies they would initiate into their programs. Finally, they were asked to tell what happened when they tried the new strategies. TRLs repeatedly described the ways in which they rearranged their classrooms, developed more realistic consequences to help enforce classroom rules, or tried to deliver praise to students in a more specific manner. Often they told us how their students reacted to these changes. In some cases, school-wide changes came about as a result of a few teachers' input on better strategies suggested from the research. In all cases, building principals were supportive of the process, having previously agreed that they would not evaluate teacher performance based on their efforts to incorporate the research strategies into their daily teaching. In most cases, principals acknowledged that they were witnessing improvement in practice by teachers in their schools, but they refrained, by agreement, from mandating implementation by all teachers.

When we discussed change in practice with TRLs, they told us that it was not always immediately clear that change had taken place; that growth in the program was necessarily a "slow process." But they were always enthusiastic about their newly acquired skills in understanding research-based concepts, being familiar with the names of educational researchers and their work, and utilizing a research vocabulary in discussing teaching techniques. These practices made the TRLs feel "special" and enhanced their professional self-esteem. One TRL told us:

> Before I became involved in this program I had begun to stop thinking. I was so accustomed to top-down decisions that I had used no effort and just coasted. Now, I feel like a professional. I've begun to make decisions and assume authority over my practice. Even my husband noticed the change.

The Educational Research and Dissemination process and the research information stood up to the test. Teachers were quite amazed to discover that there was some practical value to the information generated by the research. The teachers at one site discovered via Barak Rosenshine's Instructional Functions that the district-mandated CBC (Competency Based Curriculum) program was rooted in research. "So, that's where they got it" was their reaction. They further stated that they felt better equipped to handle the program as a result of their understanding of its research base.

Teacher Training

Implications for preservice training were consistently evident during the project funding period and continue to be of importance at the present time. In almost all situations when the research-based materials were presented, teachers reacted with, "Why didn't we get this when we were in training?" or, "This information should be given to all student teachers." Most teachers at the sites said they had not had a college course that dealt specifically with *classroom management*. They felt that such a course should be developed and presented, using the research materials. Further, they urged colleges of education to work harder to create in prospective teachers an interest in research and a desire to remain research users throughout their teaching careers. Perhaps colleges need to redirect the ways in which they teach and use research. We have discovered that the way in which the information is shared is as important as the information itself.

Teachers are largely uninformed about the infrastructure of the general education process. Most are unaware of the functions and impact of the Educational Centers and Laboratories on their professional lives. This information has never been presented to them. This is a service that could be provided to prospective teachers by the training institutions.

As far as research concepts are concerned, once the project's TRLs had accepted the research-based information, they usually asked "Who will inservice the school principals to keep them abreast of the research strategies we will be using in the classroom?" Again, colleges of education prepare administrators as well as teachers. The research influence should be firmly established during the training process. College teachers may find that they have to "bone-up" on the kinds of research that appear to have great relevance to practice and incorporate the strategies into course presentations.

Finally, colleges of education may find it to their advantage to develop greater involvement with practicing teachers. This would tend to facilitate "theory into practice" and would result in a process of mutual benefit to all concerned. Teachers will continue to need research information provided to them in usable form. Researchers, university and college staff can benefit from teacher feedback on the workability of concepts.

Collaboration
And Institutionalization

The success of the American Federation of Teachers Educational Research and Dissemination project was substantial. Teachers applied research to classroom teaching when the information was shared in a manner that was understandable, practical, and non-threatening. Since the project period netted five translated studies, it was important to establish collaborative relationships with colleges and universities at the local sites so that the supply of research would be constantly forthcoming. Deans of education from most of the major colleges in New York City, Washington, D.C., and San Francisco met with us to discuss ways of continuing the program. In every case, interest was high and funds were low. Collaborative relationships have been initiated at Fordham University, George Washington University, Stanford University, and others. Noteworthy is the relationship at Stanford where one of the San Francisco TRLs has taken sabbatical leave from teaching and is participating at Stanford as a "Distinguished Visiting Practitioner" on a tuition-free basis and is learning how to read, interpret and translate research studies. She is auditing three courses and participating with Stanford staff on a peer level. Her input as a practicing teacher is of great value to the Graduate School of Education faculty there. Funds to support her participation have been donated by the Hewlitt-Packard Foundation and AFT. Since the initiation of this process, our department has received inquiries from other major universities on how they might become involved in a similar effort. Research studies translated by this TRL will be shared with the original pilot sites, as well as with the eleven new sites now in operation in AFT locals across the country. Training for the program's new Local Site Coordinators was conducted at Skidmore College this past summer. Another training session is planned for summer 1984, when another 15 site leaders will be trained. There are approximately 150 TRLs now functioning as research resource people or in training for the role.

Conclusions

There was much to be learned in the course of the Educational Research and Dissemination process. The effectiveness of the Teacher Center model was reaffirmed by our use of the peer-to-peer training process. The teachers union can serve as an effective dissemination vehicle for transmitting professional knowledge to teachers.

Further, we were made aware of the importance of the element of time in developing and conducting the program, i.e., length of training sessions, level of acceptance, and implementation of research strategies by individual teachers. We call this process of internalization the "transformation" of research into practice.

We realized that staff development, as an on-going process, is more effective in retraining teachers than one-shot, inservice workshops.

Finally, we are assured that there is a wealth of good research on effective practice which is useful not only to practicing teachers, but also to student teachers. Research on teaching effectiveness and classroom management should be integrated into teacher education programs. Support for this conclusion has been offered by the researchers themselves who told us that they were delighted to have a mechanism through which their work was made directly accessible to teachers.

"If teaching is an activity about which we can have knowledge, is it not reasonable to contend that those who teach ought to have what knowledge is available about what it is they do?" (Fenstermacher, 1980).

The gap between research and practice need not remain permanent.

References

Brophy, J. (1981). Teacher praise: A functional analysis. *Review of Educational Research, 51,* 5-21.

Emmer, E., Evertson, C., & Anderson, L. (1980). Effective classroom management at the beginning of the school year. *The Elementary School Journal, 80,* 219-231.

Fenstermacher, G. D. (1980). On learning to teach effectively from research on teacher effectiveness. In C. Denham & A. Lieberman (Eds.), *Time to learn* (pp. 127-138). Washington, DC: Government Printing Office.

Fisher, C. W., and others. (1980). Teaching behaviors, academic learning time, and school achievement: An overview. In C. Denham & A. Lieberman (Eds.), *Time to learn* (pp. 7-32). Washington, DC: Government Printing Office.

Good, T. L., & Grouws, D. A. (1979). The Missouri mathematics effectiveness project. *Journal of Educational Psychology, 71,* 355-362.

Kidd, J. R. (1973). *How adults learn.* New York: Association Press.

Kounin, J. (1970). *Discipline and group management in classrooms.* Melabar, FL: Robert E. Krieger Publishing Company.

Rosenshine, B. V. (1980). How time is spent in elementary classrooms. In C. Denham & A. Lieberman (Eds.), *Time to learn.* Washington, DC: Government Printing Office.

Stallings, J. (1980). Allocated academic learning time revisited, or beyond time-on-task. *Educational Researcher, 9(*11), 11-16.

Weber, W. (1981). *Teacher perceptions of classroom management strategy.* Paper presented at annual meeting of the American Educational Research Association, Los Angeles, CA.

A Regional
Laboratory Works with Schools

Linda Sikorski and Robert Ewy

Mid-continent Regional Education Laboratory

The mission of the Mid-continental Regional Education Laboratory (McREL) is to improve practice and increase academic performance in the schools of the seven-state mountain-plains region. For the most part this is accomplished through the transfer and application of research-based knowledge to practice and policy settings. In particular, McREL has disseminated the "effective schools" research to schools and SEAs in the region. The coalescence of this research took place at about the same time that McREL was planning its service activities (i.e., 1978), so it quite naturally became the focus of those activities.

McREL's principal approach to the dissemination and utilization (d&u) of the effective schools research has been training. Other d&u modes have been used as well, e.g., *Noteworthy*, (an aperiodic monograph) and the State Policy Activity, but McREL's Effective Schools Program (ESP), which consists of presentations and training based on the effective schools research, represents the single most significant activity. This report is concerned with the description of the Effective Schools Program.

The Effective Schools Program: Goals, Structure, and Process

The effective schools research indicates building and classroom practices that promote student achievement, e.g., Good (1983). Because a school's resources, including time, are not unlimited, the research focuses in large part on increasing school efficiency. Based on this research, McREL's Effective Schools Program aims at providing participants with knowledge and skills to implement research-based practices, with the ultimate goals of: (1) increased school efficiency and (2) increased student achievement.

The enabling objectives of the Effective Schools Program are:

- to increase participants' understanding of the effective schools research and its applications to their situation;
- to help participants examine and select strategies based on the research to improve the performance of administrators, teachers, and students;
- to facilitate participants' development of a long-term, multi-year, building-level effective schools plan.

The training educators receive through the Effective Schools Program emphasizes data collection about current practices, training and coaching in the use of new practices, and feedback for monitoring and guiding progress. The program is designed to meet school or district improvement needs, to develop a pool of on-site training material, and to give participants the skills to train their colleagues and other staff members. In short, it provides a complete and self-sustainable program of school improvement.

School districts participating in the Effective Schools Program follow a five-part process:

1. Orientation.

The program starts with an overview of the effective schools research base and an orientation to the Effective Schools Program. It involves one or more visits by a McREL staff member to present the research and the Effective Schools Program to the superintendent, school board, and selected principals, teachers and parents. The orientation provides participants with a practical understanding of how they can make their schools and classrooms more effective, and enables them to make an informed decision about whether to commit to the Effective Schools Program.

2. Logistical Planning

Following the orientation, the planning for the Effective Schools Program takes place. The program offers units as depicted in Figure 1; schools will generally choose some, but not all, as the content for the training sessions. During this stage of the ESP, the desired assessment, training, and development activities are determined. A member of McREL's staff meets with a district or school leadership team to set objectives, plan activities and schedules, and identify participants. Costs are projected and a contract or letter of agreement is signed.

Figure 1
Units of the Effective Schools Program

File I. Instruction	File II. School Management	File IV. Change Process
A. Time	A. Effective schools	A. Instruments
B. Classroom management	B. Leadership	B. Process
C. Discipline	File III. Testing and Curriculum	File V. Technology
D. Motivation	A. Testing	
E. Expectations	B. Curriculum	
F. Instruction		
G. Beginning the school year		

156

3. Assessment and Training.

The assessment and training portions of the ESP are interdependent. The training is based in part on results of self-diagnosis by school participants, and their skills in self-diagnosis are transmitted and reinforced by the training. The assessment and training portions of the ESP are delivered to two audiences: (1) teams composed of staff and principals, and (2) school administrators, usually principals, who meet separately with the trainers. The teams usually include three or four teachers at the elementary level and seven or eight at the secondary level, in addition to the building principals. The teams from the participating schools in a district are trained in four one-day workshops (maximum attendance is 50). Workshops are scheduled at least four weeks apart so that some "at-home" activities can take place after each one. One such activity is application of the information presented during the workshop. Another is data collection. Team members observe one another's classrooms, complete instruments tapping their beliefs and perceptions, and observe their own students and record those observations. These assessments enable them to diagnose areas of strength and weakness in their teaching practices and establish an experiential context for the information provided during training.

Between team workshops, the principals meet for four half-day sessions. These meetings focus on instructional leadership and are based on data that principals collect about their own behaviors and personal leadership styles.

Handouts and worksheets distributed at the workshops are collected in a notebook and form a reference manual for participants to take with them when training is completed.

4. Improvement Planning.

The information gathered during assessment and training is used to develop a school improvement plan that addresses both short and long term needs. McREL staff lead the decision-making team through a planning activity designed to develop consensus about needed improvements and the steps that should be taken to accomplish them. Consideration is given not only to establishing priorities among alternative courses of action, but to the group dynamics involved, leadership styles, participant concerns, the needs for short-term impact, and so forth.

The improvement plan, like the diagnostic process, applies the state of the art in planned educational change. The behaviors of teachers in their classrooms, outcomes presently being achieved by students, and current school characteristics are used to produce a performance profile for the school. Discrepancies between the current profile and the school's desired performance are translated into prescriptions for change. The school improvement plan:

• specifies manageable stages of change between present and preferred outcomes and behavior,

• specifies potential obstacles to the implementation of improvement plans, and

- sets down workable strategies to overcome the identified obstacles and attain the preferred outcomes.

A McREL-designed computer software package can be used for these steps if appropriate hardware is available.

The plan includes an evaluation component for providing information on how much growth individuals are achieving, how the school is moving to match the effective school characteristics, and whether the strategies for overcoming obstacles are working.

5. Follow-up

A final phase of the Effective Schools Program provides for follow-up visits by McREL staff to assist the school in successfully implementing the effective schools plan. McREL staff monitor and assess the plan, coach, model skills, and disseminate relevant materials to support the plan.

Evaluation Design

Several features of the ESP pose constraints on assessing program impact. First, like most complex change programs, the ESP has diffuse goals and objectives. The program is intended to bring about positive change in variables it doesn't touch directly, as a cumulative effect of a series of interactions and resources that themselves represent complex training events. Conceptually, the intended impact moves through levels and stages of change as depicted in Figure 2.

Figure 2
Tracing Pattern of Desired McREL-ESP Impact

	ESP Participants	Building	Classroom	Students
Level #1	Research ESP Design workshops — changes in knowledge, awareness, perceptions, skills			
Level #2	changes in behavior on-site			
Level #3		changes in the building culture		
Level #4			changes in classrooms	
Level #5				changes in student motivation, engag., success rates, etc.
Level #6				changes in student achievement

   The ESP operates in a change environment that is even more complex. At any given time, the program is only one of a myriad of factors influencing the knowledge, perceptions, beliefs, and behaviors of participants. And, a direct outcome of the program is only one of many factors influencing what may ultimately occur in the classrooms and buildings in question.

   Because of this complexity, McREL does not attempt to experimentally isolate the intended effects of the ESP. Rather, McREL recognizes that positive changes and interesting patterns of effect may be "contaminated" and/or diluted by non-ESP occurrences. Additionally, some effects may not be captured by our assessment instruments. Our solution is to examine the *weight* of available evidence across sites and measures. That is, McREL seeks to show that despite the variability of contexts, certain effects and changes appear most or all of the time where we are able to measure them.

A second constraint on evaluating the ESP is McREL's desire to refrain from placing too great a response burden on participants. Assessment requirements of the program itself, without additional impact assessment, probably approach participants' upper limits of tolerance. They are "paying customers" in most cases, and are not always amenable to providing data not needed for the training. For this reason, our impact assessment relies on the data produced through training rather than on additional data gathered solely for evaluation purposes. Also, we use an unbalanced matrix, pre-experimental sampling design; each of the data sources used is available from only a subsample of sites, selected in part on the basis of their willingness to provide the information we need. Again, McREL relies on weight of evidence, or triangulation, rather than a pure experimental effect, to inform us about what the ESP is accomplishing.

An additional feature of the program reinforces the choice of a non-probability sampling approach; that is, the treatment or intervention is fluid, and in some respects, changeable. Trainers intentionally adapt their efforts to the idiosyncracies of sites and participant groups, rather than treating all sites the same. Within bounds, the trainers differ in the approaches they use, emphasizing those they do best. The program itself is tailored to the needs and goals at each site; essentially, each site receives a custom program. And, the ESP is constantly evolving to accommodate and/or capitalize on new research findings, newly-discovered training approaches, new areas of interest. Thus, the external validity of evaluation results from a sample of sites. Even a "representative" sample of sites is somewhat questionable. We try instead to gather evidence across as many sites as possible, and draw conclusions from the weight of that evidence.

Summary

McREL believes that as the body of research on school and teacher effectiveness merge, we are moving closer to a firm science of school improvement and that this science provides a good framework for designing school development activities. With over 100 individual schools and school districts, including rural isolated, suburban, urban, elementary, junior-middle, and high schools in 14 states, completing The Effective Schools Program, evidence supports the validity of this approach to improve the efficiency, the effectiveness, and most importantly, the relevance of what goes on in schools to achieve high levels of student academic success.

References

Good, T. L. (Ed.). (1983). Research on teaching [Special issue]. *The Elementary School Journal, 83*(4).

Summaries of Consortium
Team Plans to Utilize Research
In Teacher Education

CHADRON STATE COLLEGE

Pat Colgate
Roger Wess
Al Holst

Chadron State College is located in the extreme northwest corner of Nebraska. It is 100 miles from Rapid City, South Dakota; 100 miles from Scottsbluff, Nebraska and 450 miles from Lincoln, Nebraska. The on-campus enrollment is usually 1,200 students and the off-campus enrollment is about 600. Education majors comprise about one third of the undergraduate enrollment and almost all of the graduate enrollment. The college students are primarily from western Nebraska and eastern Wyoming. Most students and faculty are those who are drawn to a small community and a rural environment.

Chadron State was a normal school, then a teachers college and finally a liberal arts college with a strong emphasis on teacher education programs. Chadron works with students in small classes and closely coordinates the different aspects of its teacher education programs. This has allowed the college to develop a reputation for graduating very professional and competent teachers. The emphasis on research in teaching should help the program do better what it does well already.

The first goal is to formally determine the research base already taught in Chadron teacher education programs. The next step is to update and emphasize the use of research findings in our programs. Finally, a determination will be made as to whether the graduates have improved because of the research emphasis.

The plan is to accomplish much of this work over the next spring and fall semester. There will be a series of meetings with the Education Committee and the Education Faculty to explain the thrust of this program, determine what is presently being done and survey the research in the various subject areas. Research will be emphasized in the subject matter areas, general methods and student teaching.

Chadron State is presently evaluating its teacher education programs in light of the analyses and criticisms contained in the many recent reports on education. The emphasis of the use of research information in teacher education will be an integral part of this overall review.

COLLEGE OF SAINT MARY

Gayle Schou
Karen Scheerer

The College of Saint Mary, founded in 1923 by the Sisters of Mercy, is a private, independent Catholic institution located in Omaha which has an integrated liberal arts component combined with professional and career preparation. The mission of CSM is to be a facilitator in the lifelong learning process aimed at the liberation and humanization of persons in an atmosphere which frees them to grow. The majority of students are from Nebraska and Iowa. College of Saint Mary enrollment also includes students from 14 other states and from ten foreign countries.

The Early Childhood Education and the Elementary and Secondary Education are part of the Education/Business Division and two of the twenty-six departments at College of Saint Mary. The Education Department is approved to offer work leading to teacher certification in elementary and secondary education by the State Department of Public Instruction in both Nebraska and Iowa.

Beginning with their first semester freshman course in education, Introduction to Education, students work in classrooms or early childhood settings. Many opportunities are planned for College of Saint Mary students to experiment with and practice a variety of teaching styles, through the more than 300 hours of field experiences that are provided in the four-year program. The junior year is termed the "professional year" when students attend method classes off-campus in field-based experiences for Language Arts, Social Studies, Science, Reading, Math, Music, Art, Health and Physical Education. College of Saint Mary seniors spend a complete semester in the role of student teacher. They experience two separate placements, at two different grade levels, to increase the student's exposure to teaching philosophies and cultural backgrounds, and teaching styles.

The first goal of CSM's plan is to develop more rigorous standards for admission into the teacher education program which students apply for after the Fall semester of their sophomore year. Beginning in 1985 these standards will be:

1) Administering the Pre-Professional Skills Test instead of the previously used department-made test. The PPST would be used as a diagnostic tool and if necessary, remediation would be prescribed.

2) Taking a spontaneous writing sample when the PPST is taken. The writing sample would be assessed for clarity, content, and accuracy.

3) Having an admission interview with education faculty members, and representatives from the Education Committee and the Education Advisory Committee to assess speech, presentation, poise, as well as aspiration and sincerity. The admission standards would still include the 2.5 quality point average, recommendations from faculty mem-

bers who have had the student in class, and the completion of three full semesters of EDU 101.

The second goal involves curriculum changes. The following changes have already been approved by the Curriculum Committee and voted on by the College of Saint Mary faculty:

1) Including an Introduction to Early Childhood Education course.
2) Adding Early Childhood Education Methods II for three credit hours.
3) Issuing of two grades for the student teaching course, to reflect the two separate grade-level experiences students have.

The following courses are still in the planning stage and probably will not be part of the College of Saint Mary curriculum until 1986 or later:

1) Course on classroom management.
2) Course on tests and measurements for the classroom teacher.
3) Course in the use of audiovisual materials and computer software in education.

A third goal is the all-around upgrading of Education courses to reflect current research in teacher effectiveness. We anticipate purchasing the video-tapes, Effective Teaching for Higher Achievement offered by the Association for Supervision and Curriculum Development, which feature researchers such as David Berliner, Jere Brophy, Carolyn Evertson, Tom Good, Penelope Peterson, Barak Rosenshine, and Jane Stallings. These tapes will be used in Introduction to Education and other appropriate methods courses.

A final goal, which is still in the pre-planning stage, is a plan to match student teachers with teachers who are master teachers in their field and who know and implement the research on teacher effectiveness, or who are willing to work through College of Saint Mary to acquire the knowledge.

CONCORDIA TEACHERS COLLEGE

Marvin Bergman
Glenn Einspahr
Carl Everts
Priscilla Lawin
Eugene Oetting
Douglas Woltemath

Concordia Teachers College is owned and operated by the Lutheran Church - Missouri Synod. Concordia's foremost goal is the education of the whole person for effective Christian living and for ministry to church and world. This goal is accomplished through baccalaureate degree programs in professional education and liberal arts. Approximately two-thirds of the 900+ student body is enrolled in teacher education. The other one-third of the student body's enrollment is divided among the pre-seminary, director of Christian education, social work, medical theology, business and pre-profes-sional studies for law and medicine.

The general goal of Concordia's Consortium Team is to increase both awareness and use of appropriate research on instruction in the college's teacher education program. Specific goals are:

1. To have the consortium team members become more familiar with the research that was presented at the workshop,
2. To include some of the research on instruction which was recommended or presented at the Consortium workshop, in the Education and Psychology courses taught by Concordia's team members as appropriate to the purposes of those courses,
3. To make sure that research findings on instruction are being utilized in a sufficient number of required courses to reach all Concordia teacher education program students.

The procedure to be used in an attempt to reach the general and specific goals will include the following steps:

1. Regular meetings of Concordia's Consortium Team will be established for the second semester of the 1983-84 school year. A schedule for presenting written and oral summaries of selected research on instruction to the total team will be drafted and assignments for each team member will be designated.
2. Team members will study and receive reports on the current research on instruction to determine which portions seem appropriate for their respective courses, including student teaching. Then they will begin incorporating the selected research into their courses.
3. A questionnaire will be used to gather data on where current research on instruction is being utilized in selected required Education and Psychology courses, including student teaching.
4. The Concordia Consortium Team will prepare a recommendation(s) concerning what should be added to selected Education and Psychology courses to provide all Concordia teacher education students with knowledge of and experience with current research on instruction.

Ultimately the Concordia team envisions that some type of student evaluation will also be devised. Such an evaluation should measure the extent to which current research on instruction has become a part of Concordia's teacher education students' knowledge base, classroom planning processes and teaching strategies.

CREIGHTON UNIVERSITY

Edward O'Connor
Larry Johnson
Paul Hartnett
Della Bonner

Creighton University is a Jesuit, Catholic, and urban institution of higher education. Enrollment in the fall semester of 1983 was 6,301. Creighton's student body is cosmopolitan with students coming from 49 states and 27 foreign countries. The average ACT score of freshmen who entered in 1983 was 23.1. The University includes the College of Arts and Sciences, College of Business Administration, Schools of Dentistry, Medicine, Law, Nursing, Pharmacy, and Graduate School. The Education Department is one of nineteen departments in the College of Arts and Sciences.

Teacher education programs at Creighton University are designed to meet the goals of the University, the College of Arts and Sciences, and the Education Department. The programs are intended to prepare professional educators who:

1. can recognize, identify, and be sensitive to the needs of all students and our society;
2. can select and employ strategies for making decisions regarding instructional and educational programs while holding concern for the student's welfare to be paramount;
3. can work cooperatively with colleagues, educational representatives, and members of the community;
4. can work effectively and creatively in meeting the needs of many situations with varied contexts in our rapidly changing society;
5. can promote growth in students (mental, physical, emotional, and social) and in the community they serve; and
6. are interested in scholarship, continued training, renewal and research that relates to becoming more proficient in their professional role.

A. Creighton's Consortium goals are:
1. to improve the elementary and secondary methods courses by correlating (a) the method of instruction given with (b) observation of this method actually being used in elementary and secondary school classrooms in the metropolitan area by master teachers. Students should be better able to understand the rationale for the type of method taught when they witness the same process in a "live" classroom. (Methods courses are taken in the junior year and application by these students is not possible until the senior year during student teaching.)
2. to improve student teaching during the senior year by increasing the correlation between methods taught and those observed during the junior year.

3. to develop a closer working relationship between University instructors who teach methods courses and practitioners in the field.
B. Steps to be taken are:
  1. Meet with instructors who teach methods courses to arrange for the implementation of the plan which includes: (a) agree on which schools and which master teachers should be used; (b) meet with University instructors and practitioners to explain the plan; (c) put the plan into operation during school year 1984-85; (d) establish methods for determining the effectiveness of the plan.
C. The intended result is an improvement in the instruction process so that methods courses will have greater significance to the students taking them.

DANA COLLEGE

Ray Weckmuller
Bernard Matthies
Dorothy Olson
Shirley McAllister

Dana College is one of thirteen colleges owned and operated by The American Lutheran Church. Dana is located in Blair, Nebraska and has approximately 500 students. One-third of the student body is committed to teacher education, the largest professional program of the college. Other areas of study include: social work, business administration, accounting and pre-professional.

Faculty of Dana College believe that there is a continuing need in our society for public school teachers who are sincerely dedicated to serving others. We believe that the type of student who seeks an education in a church-related college such as Dana is particularly well suited to this task. The faculty and staff of Dana College have long been committed to providing a quality program of teacher education.

The goal of Dana's project is to structure the professional sequence of courses in its teacher education program in such a way that every student will experience instruction in each of several selected teaching models.

Each teacher education student will be able to explain the theoretical base of each of the selected models.

Each education student will demonstrate proficiency in teaching each of the selected models in a micro-teaching setting.

Steps to be taken in developing the project are as follows.
1. Review the research dealing with specific teaching models.
2. Identify models to be used.
3. Identify models currently being used in the Dana professional sequence.
4. Assign selected models not currently being used by staff members.

5. Develop materials explaining the research base of each model.
6. Develop a flow chart indicating where each model is being utilized.

The Dana project evolved from the session conducted by Alvah Kilgore. It is based on the assumption that teachers should have a broad repertoire of teaching models. There is a general perception that teacher educators seldom "practice what they teach." While we doubt that this perception is very accurate, this project will insure that our teacher education students will be knowledgeable about the research base and methodology of each model selected and will have experienced instruction under each model.

DOANE COLLEGE

Lowell Dodd
Kay Hegler
Paulie Mills
Julie Kozisek
Richard Dudley

Doane College is a private, independent and coeducational residential college which offers undergraduate instruction leading to the Bachelor of Arts degree in the liberal arts and related professional and pre-professional areas. The educational program is student centered and characterized by close student-teacher relationships. The college views its primary mission to be preparation of students for life as well as preparation to make a living through the acquisition of life-long functional and intellectual skills as defined in the Doane Plan of education. The educational program serves a student body which is largely of traditional college age and midwestern, with a majority from Nebraska. Through its 110 year history Doane has continued to view, as part of its mission, the training of teachers. Approximately 35% of the 650 students are intending to be certified in elementary, secondary or special education.

Since 1970 Doane's teacher education program has been competency-based. A field component which involves every student in a classroom for 350 hours prior to student teaching provides the practical setting in which the student develops the required competencies. Beginning in 1981 Doane moved to an extended program which requires the students to complete twelve graduate credits, through a cooperative program with the University of Nebraska–Lincoln, in the summer following their graduation from Doane. These twelve credits are required for certification. This extended program also requires Doane faculty to visit the beginning teacher in his/her classroom during the first weeks of teaching to provide a support system for the beginning teacher.

Doane College's Action Plan includes the following goals:

1. Make some decisions about what we want students to learn about research in their undergraduate education.
2. Investigate the body of teacher effectiveness research and seek ways to implement this body of knowledge into Practicum I. (Practicum I is the core experience in education which all students must complete.)
3. Integrate the information which is required of students in Practicum I into Practica II, III, IV and V. (Practicum II is the methods courses; Practicum III is the student teaching; Practicum IV is the graduate experience at UN-L in the summer following the student's graduation; and Practicum V is the integrated experience in the student's first year of teaching.)
4. Identify specific journals and monographs to be added to the library and the education staff collections.

To accomplish those goals, the Doane faculty will need to undertake several activities.

Our faculty is not knowledgeable about much of the material which will be implemented for this project. We have not spent time reading research articles. Our initial step will be to have individual faculty do a range of reading and to share the information. We will prepare a bibliography and will consult with the Dean and the Librarian about funds for providing these materials. We intend to complete this phase by April 1. Prior to May 15, the faculty will make some decisions about revision of Practicum I materials to implement our second Goal. We will not revise the materials in Practicum II, III, IV and V until late in 1984 or early in 1985 when we can evaluate the Practicum I experience. Our primary focus will be on Practicum I for all students.

We are primarily interested in expanding our students' knowledge base in management, planning, decision-making and other teacher effectiveness research and their ability to apply the information they gather in their teacher assisting experience as well as their other field experiences. (Every student in Practicum I spends a minimum of 300 hours in a classroom as a teaching assistant.) We believe that if we give them a solid introduction in their Practicum I experience and build on this throughout their other experiences, they will carry the habit of utilizing research in their experience as a teacher with them into the profession.

HASTINGS COLLEGE

Ladd Cochrane
Don Goodrich
Jan Watkins
Mel-Elaine Krutz

Hastings College is a Presbyterian Church related Liberal Arts institution located in Hastings, Nebraska, a city of 23,000. The majority of the student body, who come from twenty one states and six foreign countries, are housed on campus where they are taught by a faculty with over fifty percent earned doctorates and with a student-teacher ratio of thirteen to one. Seventy percent of the student body come from Nebraska and the majority of the teacher education graduates are placed in Nebraska schools. Graduates are in high demand and justify the department's assertion that we have no difficulty placing graduates who will go where the jobs are.

The Education Department Faculty consists of five persons. Department courses range from the usual methods courses for the classroom to specialty courses ranging from exceptionality of gifted, retarded, and learning disabled to reading in the content field, supervision in laboratory, clinical and practicum programs. Methods for K-12 endorsements in Art, Music and Physical Education as well as all other secondary courses are taught by the major departments. Fourteen departments offer endorsements in teacher education.

The Hastings College intent in the Consortium is to bring cooperating teachers, departmental methods teachers, supervising teachers, and student teachers in direct and indirect contact with currently available education research.

The Hastings College action plan has three major activities: 1) Department time will be devoted to Education Faculty in-service in the form of reporting abstracts and research models; 2) the Department will publish a newsletter which, among other things, will summarize or abstract pieces of cogent research related to classroom/learning performance; 3) workshops/courses for cooperating teachers will be taught by teams from the department to highlight educational research.

Hastings College will emphasize learning models that can be applied, with the consent of the classroom teacher and building principal, in the classrooms where the college places its clinical (second level) and practicum (student students. In addition the team plans to share, in a nonthreatening way, research models and results with departmental methods teachers for their evaluation and consideration in their methods classes.

Hastings will concentrate primarily on field experiences but with an implied crossover into the methods courses.

RESULTS OF EFFORTS:

1. An effective and professionally valuable in-service program along the education staff itself.
2. We believe, as we attack the reservations that we observe among class-room teachers about applying innovative ideas with supportive research and viable approaches, that we will be providing a vital sense of direction and vision toward excellence in education. That should be expected of any institution that is serious about training teachers.
3. We expect to fortify a more supportive public relations image with area educators and the public in general, as well as our alumni.
4. We intend to improve the practice of teaching by the utilization of research and the body of specific knowledge that supports good teaching.

NEBRASKA WESLEYAN UNIVERSITY

Art Nicolai
Larry Vaughan
Lois Coleman
Betty Grassmeyer
Ila Dean Horn

Nebraska Wesleyan University is a four-year undergraduate, private, independent college. The University maintains a mutually supportive relationship with the Nebraska Annual Conference of the United Methodist Church. About 1,200 students are enrolled.

The campus of 50 acres is located in Northeast Lincoln, Nebraska. The University's first building, Old Main (1888) remains in use and is listed on the National Register of Historic Landmarks.

Nebraska Wesleyan is accredited by leading regional and national accrediting agencies for its academic program. Nationally, it is approved by the University Senate of the United Methodist Church, the National Council for the Accreditation of Teacher Education, The American Association of Colleges for Teacher Education, the National Association of Schools of Music, and The American Chemical Society.

The action plan that the Nebraska Wesleyan University team devised at the consortium was to investigate research in the area of admission, retention and exit standards for teacher education programs, to assist the university in revising its standards of admission, retention, and exit.

The university intends to use an ERIC search as its original source of information. From the ERIC search the team will refine and develop a procedure for reviewing specific research findings with the intention to incorporate the findings into new admission, retention, and exit standards for the Teacher Education Program.

PERU STATE COLLEGE

Esther Divney
Jack Hytrek
Paul Mars

Peru State was founded in 1867 and is the oldest college in Nebraska and the third oldest teacher-training institution established west of the Missouri River. Peru was founded the same year Nebraska became a state.

The mission of Peru State College is to offer instruction in selected programs and courses of study, to conduct research, and to provide public service. Instructional programs include teacher education, liberal arts, sciences, pre-professional curricula, occupational and continuing education.

Peru State College is committed to the belief that all citizens are endowed with potential abilities which, if discovered and developed, will reflect to the benefit of that individual and to the populace at large. Those who are exposed to the influence of the college are encouraged to develop those potentials and concurrently encouraged to develop understanding of and appreciation of the contributions made by others.

In consideration of the teacher education program at Peru State College, the team identified four areas of concern. Through work with faculty, administration and students we will attempt to:

1. develop a more rigorous standard for admission into the teacher education program.
2. identify procedures for the maintenance of high standards in the teacher education program.
3. develop additional field experience to be included in the teacher education program.
4. Develop additional criteria for the identification and evaluation of prospective teacher certification candidates.

We will work with faculty in the Division of Education and Psychology, the Teacher Education Committee, the Academic Affairs Commission, and the College Affairs Council. It has been suggested that an advisory board consisting of Superintendents, Principals, and Teachers be established. With the combined effort of the membership of these groups, we will develop a consensus for Teacher Education Program change at Peru State College.

Our time line for work relative to change in the teacher education program at Peru State College will be:

1. Division of Education and Psychology - January
2. Education and Psychology Advisory Board - On-going
3. Teacher Education Committee - February
4. Academic Affairs Committee - March
5. College Affairs Council - April

UNION COLLEGE

Charles E. Felton
Ben Bandiola
Aleene Schaeffer
Virginia Simmons

Union College is an independent, four-year, coeducational college of liberal arts and sciences, owned and operated by the Seventh-Day Adventist Church. Although basically a liberal arts college, it seeks to fulfill its mission by offering programs designed to prepare students for such professions as business, nursing, teaching, and theology. Union also offers pre-professional programs which prepare students to pursue their education for such professions as gospel ministry, medicine, law, dentistry, and other helping professions. Union was the first Seventh-Day Adventist college to be NCATE accredited (1963). The fourth re-accreditation was granted in 1983 with strengths cited in three areas.

The student body of Union College is cosmopolitan; seventy-five percent of the students come from the nine state constituency in Mid-America which includes Minnesota, Iowa, Missouri, North Dakota, South Dakota, Nebraska, Kansas, Wyoming, and Colorado. Twelve percent come from twenty-four countries, with the highest number coming from Canada, Malaysia, and Japan. The remaining thirteen percent come from other states outside the nine state constituency.

Union College has always endorsed the concept that there is a body or core of knowledge which all graduates should have and that its curriculum must be constantly reviewed to keep it congruent with the college's mission and goals. For the college that is church affiliated, there are unique characteristics of doctrine and philosophy to which the sponsoring group give strong support in the curriculum design. Students are urged to develop the tools of independent thought and expression which provides a matrix for responsible, creative, and adaptive participation in a rapidly changing society. The college endeavors to foster active integration of faith with learning and culture, and maximum academic achievement with dedication to service.

The two-fold goal developed in the action plan includes the following:
1. To increase the repertoire of pre-service teachers by exposing candidates to instruction in a wider variety of the following;
   a. Models and methods of effective teaching
   b. Classroom management skills derived from research
   c. Effective allocation and utilization of instructional time.
2. To develop and implement plans for "translation" of research in the above-mentioned areas in classroom practice.

As a part of regular program review and update, the professional education sequence of both elementary and secondary curricula is undergoing reorganization. This activity will continue with added emphasis on the integration of relevant research into the program. This reorganization effort will lead to:

1. Identification of the relevant courses;
2. Description of the content of these courses;
3. Determination of the sequence of these courses.

The three areas of research identified in the goal statements will be examined. The program components that will be specifically affected by this reorganization effort are (a) foundations and education-related science courses and (b) methods courses.

The intended result of these efforts will be improved classroom performance of teacher candidates as initially observed in their student teaching program and subsequently gathered from follow-up studies of graduates, based on their self-perception of their teacher effectiveness and reports of their principals and supervisors. Feedback from these follow-up studies will again serve as bases for on-going improvement efforts.

UNIVERSITY OF NEBRASKA-LINCOLN

Joe Aguilar
Clarise Ramsey
Toni Santmire
Jane Stewart

Jill Stoefen-Fisher

The University of Nebraska-Lincoln (UN-L) is a comprehensive state university that enrolls approximately 25,000 students, ninety percent from Nebraska and ten percent from the forty-nine other states and seventy-five foreign countries. Within the University, Teachers College is responsible for the education of undergraduate and graduate students who will become teachers, counselors and administrators in public and private schools in Nebraska and surrounding states. The College offers more than 40 different specialties in classroom teaching leading to certification. By working closely with public and parochial schools, Teachers College has developed a program that permits its students to gain classroom experience early in their University studies. This program gives students an opportunity to know both the satisfactions and the pressures of the classroom atmosphere before they enroll in the more traditional psychology and methods courses.

The college is a center for educational research and investigation. The outcomes from these efforts are put to use in the instructional programs, in the development of curriculum materials, and in service to the total educational effort both within and outside the state.

The goal of this plan is to incorporate the research on classroom management into the total ongoing undergraduate teacher preparation program at the University in such a way as to improve our students' ability to be effective classroom managers. This goal was arrived at using a "practical argument" which contained the following steps:

1) Classroom management is an integral part of teaching.
2) Teaching is frustrating when the classroom is poorly managed.
3) Teachers need to be able to make their own decisions about classroom management on a day-to-day basis.
4) Teachers can be trained to be effective classroom managers.
5) Therefore, classroom management should be a part of teacher training which is given systematic attention.

The UN-L team used the model described by Ewy as the basis for planning the steps being recommended for meeting this goal. First, we intend to implement an "Academic Efficiency Audit" to ascertain just what part of the research being discussed is currently incorporated in the ongoing program. Based on the results of this audit, the staff development needs of the faculty will be assessed. Based on this assessment, the papers and/or presentations from the Consortium Workshop will be used in providing inservice for the faculty of the undergraduate program.

UN-L will hold a workshop this spring for undergraduate teacher education faculty and some cooperating teachers. The workshop will parallel the Consortium Workshop in that it will include both (1) presentations of research information and suggestions for implementation and (2) teams that will plan program modifications. However, the UN-L workshop will differ in two major respects from the one held by the Consortium: (1) research presenters will serve as direct resources to planning teams in helping them to decide what material to include and where and how to do so; (2) each team will prepare a preliminary plan for the inclusion of research information and a specific action plan for doing so, including a time line.

We will then monitor progress through an examination of course materials and assess the impact of exposure to this research on the evaluation of our student teachers.

UNIVERSITY OF NEBRASKA AT OMAHA

Larry Albertson
Carl Ashbaugh
Harl Jarmin
Ed Sadler
Kenneth Smith

The University of Nebraska at Omaha is a public institution, one of the three major campuses of the University of Nebraska. The University primarily serves the metropolitan Omaha area. The College of Education is composed of four units: the departments of Teacher Education, Counseling and Special Education, Educational Administration and Supervision, and the School of Health, Physical Education and Recreation.

The goals of the project are to:

1. Increase the research base and content in undergraduate and graduate programs and courses.
2. Utilize more research in several existing activities.
3. Utilize research in improving student teaching.
4. Increase faculty awareness of existing research in teacher education.

These goals will be reached through the inclusion of a stronger research base in several existing activities. The education courses required of all students in the College are currently under examination. This study will consider the implications of the literature for course content, methodology, etc., as well as specific research for content.

Regularly scheduled faculty colloquia will focus on research topics in teacher education and implications for various aspects of the professional preparation program. Also, selected topics of concern in teacher education will be identified for an in-depth literature review as a base for program evaluation. Topics tentatively identified for further study include classroom management, instructional time, models of teaching and characteristics of effective classrooms.

The long-term goal of the project is to increase the infusion of research into the undergraduate and graduate programs of the College to the extent that research is valued and used as an integral component of the teaching/learning process by faculty, students and graduates.

WAYNE STATE COLLEGE

Arnold Emry
Robert Bower
Herbert Root

Wayne State College is one of four state colleges in Nebraska. Almost one-half of the 2500 students are in teacher education, including undergraduate degree programs and graduate degree, inservice, and endorsement programs. Practical experiences are arranged primarily in eastern Nebraska, and most graduates accept in-state teaching positions.

Wayne State College plans to focus its Consortium activities on undergraduate programs of study leading to elementary, secondary, and K-12 teaching endorsements. All courses in those programs that are taught by Division of Education and Psychology faculty will be examined. This includes the professional studies component in all three areas and most of the endorsement requirements in elementary education, special education, and psychology.

The goal of the Wayne State College Consortium representatives is to act as a catalyst within the Division to examine the extent to which the research base supports: (a) what we teach college students to do in elementary and secondary classrooms; and (b) what we as teacher educators do to prepare college students for teaching careers. The first of these is the primary goal. The Consortium activities will be integrated with those of a comprehensive Division self-study to which the College is already committed.

The steps to be taken are as follows:

1. Examine course content by generating a list of statements for each course expressing what students are expected to know and prior learning on which those expectations depend;
2. Analyze the lists for duplication, omission, and sequence of material and make refinements accordingly;
3. Judge content according to the extent to which it reflects current research findings;
4. Prioritize content areas that should be examined in light of the research base;
5. Study the literature in content areas in order of priority;
6. Report findings to the faculty; and
7. Adjust content and methods accordingly.

Wayne State College hopes to initiate an ongoing program of self-scrutiny and subsequent refinement and have made a strong long-term commitment to integrating the research base into the curriculum. The activities described in Steps 5-7 above will be cyclical, studying a single area at a time, reporting to the faculty, and making appropriate content adjustments. Specific topics will be studied by groups of two or three faculty members with relevant responsibility, interest, and prior expertise. Proposed vehicles for reporting research findings, discussing those findings, and considering content adjustments include occasional retreats and monthly faculty forums.

The intended results of these efforts are up-to-date and intelligently sequenced curricula in undergraduate programs of study that lead to teaching endorsements. Content will reflect modern research findings, considered opinion, and prevailing practice and will be identified to students accordingly. Course and program interdependencies will be identified and addressed by adjusting content.

Notes on Contributors

LOVELY BILLUPS is Assistant Director, Educational Issues Department, American Federation of Teachers. She has been both a teacher and a leader in translating research for use by classroom teachers. She has worked nationwide in improving inservice education for teachers through the use of research information.

ROGER BRUNING is professor of Educational Psychology at the University of Nebraska–Lincoln. His research interest has focused on the development of cognitive processes through instruction and he is currently involved in field studies of the role of background knowledge and interests in reading performance. He teaches courses in cognition and instruction, the psychology of reading, and research design.

ROBERT L. EGBERT is George W. Holmes Professor of Education and former dean of Teachers College, University of Nebraska–Lincoln. His research interests include improvement of teacher education, and the impact of federal policy and programs on education. His long-range goal is that knowledge derived from both research and practice are used to improve the quality of instruction.

ROBERT EWY is Director of State Policy at the Mid-continent Regional Education Laboratory. His major research and development interests have been in the areas of school and teacher effectiveness and educational change. His work at McREL has included involvement in a multi-state effort called the Effective Schools Program, a program of activities to help educators use research to improve school effectiveness.

GARY D FENSTERMACHER is professor of Educational Foundations and Director of the Northern Virginia Graduate Center, Virginia Polytechnic Institute and State University. His research interests include the philosophy of social sciences, educational policy analysis, and research on teaching and teacher education. His participation in the Nebraska Symposium is the result of co-chairing (with Robert Egbert) the N.I.E. Project on the Improvement of Preservice Teacher Education.

PATRICIA FRIESEN is a graduate student in Educational Psychology at the University of Nebraska–Lincoln, and has taught developmental psychology in the undergraduate teacher education program. She has experience teaching junior high school students, and her research interests focus on the relationship of junior high school curriculum to the developmental characteristics of adolescents, with particular emphasis on writing.

ALVAH KILGORE is associate professor of Administration, Curriculum and Instruction at the University of Nebraska–Lincoln. His areas of specialization are instruction and supervision processes and research. He has twenty years of experience in public schools as a teacher, administrator and instructional and curriculum specialist. He currently serves as Executive Director of the Nebraska Association for Supervision and Curriculum Development.

MARY M. KLUENDER is assistant professor of Curriculum and Instruction and Coordinator of Grant Development in Teachers College, University of Nebraska–Lincoln. Her research interests include improvement of teacher education, and policy research in education.

TONI E. SANTMIRE is associate professor and Chair, Department of Educational Psychology at the University of Nebraska–Lincoln. Her major area of research interest is in how knowledge of the processes involved in psychological development can be used to provide appropriate environments for learning and development for children and adolescents, with particular emphasis on teaching writing and undergraduate teacher education.

LINDA SIKORSKI is a Principal Investigator at the Mid-continent Regional Educational Laboratory. Her major research work has focused on communication and educational change.

JANE A. STALLINGS is professor of education at George Peabody College, Vanderbilt University. Much of her research has been in the areas of effective schools and practices of effective teachers, and she has conducted staff development activities nationwide on improving classroom practice. As a faculty member in an undergraduate teacher education program, she is currently involved in incorporating some of the same research into teacher education.

STANLEY VASA is professor of Special Education in the Department of Special Education and Communications Disorders at the University of Nebraska–Lincoln. The focus of his research has been upon accomodating school programs and the environment in regular schools to the needs of mildly handicapped students, and the role of indirect consultation services in meeting the needs of mildly handicapped students.

L. JAMES WALTER is associate professor in Curriculum and Instruction at the University of Nebraska–Lincoln. His research interests include curriculum planning and change, and instructional planning and decision making. He is currently investigating the relationships between curriculum which secondary school aged students experience and the educational outcomes students attain.